ALPHA ASSERTIVENESS GUIDE FOR MEN AND WOMEN

The Workbook for Training Assertive Behavior and Communication Skills to Live Boldly, Command Respect, and Gain Confidence at Work and in Relationships

Gerard Shaw

FREE GIFT

This book includes a bonus booklet. Download may be for a limited time only. All information on how you can secure your gift right now can be found at the end of this book.

TABLE OF CONTENTS

INTRODUCTION

You want better things in life. Perhaps a better salary, higher social status, or more respect from the people around you. You want your today to be better than yesterday, and tomorrow to be better than today. And you deserve it. Really!

Not because you have been dreaming of it for so long, but also because you've been working hard to achieve it. Yet, you somehow miss the train every time. You constantly ask yourself what it is you're lacking. Or is it just bad luck?

Bad luck? Hardworking people are the creators of their own destiny, and you are not an exception. You're also an all-around nice person, very genuine and kind.

So, why aren't you getting what you deserve?

Maybe you are too generous, and your generosity is working against you. Or perhaps you never ask for what you really want, or you're unsure how to ask for it. All this, when added up, is preventing you from achieving what you desire in life, and what you deserve.

Nevertheless, it doesn't mean you can't get it NOW! You can, without losing your self-identity, your generosity, or your self-respect.

You only need to discover the most effective way to communicate and express what you want in your relationships, at work, with your family, friends, and life. Sound tough?

In this book, you'll find the blueprint of an effective communication style that equips you with the skills of expressing, asking, and receiving what you want in life. Best part?

The lessons imparted in this book are actionable and adaptable to your everyday life. It is easy to identify situations you can relate to and apply the knowledge you will learn in your day-to-day life.

I have been studying different communication techniques and picking out a select few that will equip anyone to be a winner in their life. And I mean anyone. The assertive style of communication has always stood out among the many approaches and styles of effectively communicating towards success. I have been using this communication style every day, and now have a better understanding of how it is best executed in each aspect of my life: work, relationships, family, friends, and personal development.

To tell the truth, I feel empowered in every aspect of my life when I started being more aware of using a more assertive style of communication. I feel a constantly increasing power to have more control over my life.

And now, I want you to experience the same! I want you to seize control of your life; to be empowered to control your life situations.

Reading this book will take you on a unique journey where you discover a new self. You will work with your strengths rather than lamenting your weaknesses. It will shift your entire perspective to what you *can* do to achieve what you have been aiming for.

It will give you a balanced perspective of your life, a solid idea of the know-how, and essential techniques to achieve what you want in your life through assertive behavior and communication. It will guide you through understanding assertiveness in the right context, the skills to use it appropriately in your personal life, and some workable techniques to develop these skills of communication into an empowered lifestyle.

If you ask me one thing I can share from my expertise as a communication coach that will help you lead a happier and more fulfilled life, I will tell you to discover the power of an assertive style of communication to express your wants and needs. I always advise people looking to learn effective communication skills to learn this.

Imagine the people getting that pay raise or promotion after applying the techniques they learned. Or, the couple whose marital success can be attributed to the style of communication they learned here. These are only some success stories I heard. What will your success story look like after reading this book? Imagine it- and share it with me. I eagerly await it.

Also, I promise that whatever you imagined will soon be a reality, provided you follow this blueprint. Along this path, you'll gain knowledge, wisdom, and the art of building your power. Not your physical power, but the inner potent power of assertiveness. This may be the only power you lack right now to get the life you want.

The lessons you'll learn along this journey will give you techniques to look inward, discover your strengths, and feel empowered. It will teach you how to use assertiveness to reach your end goals, whether in relationships, business, career, or just in everyday life.

The big question is: Why should you learn the assertive style of communication? The answer lies in the life situations where you currently feel you are stuck. Or might be stuck soon, if you don't learn these communication techniques now.

You may be feeling frustrated with your job, health, relationships, or financial security – that's enough to make you wonder what's wrong.

If you really wish to move ahead and stop feeling stuck in life, you need to take action today. You already know deep in your mind that something needs to change, and that change must happen now.

It's high time you stopped playing victim to your circumstances. It's time to be the master of your own destiny. If it doesn't happen now, it probably won't much later. So, get up and get ready to take charge of your life. Speak up and stand up for yourself and take the first step. Learn how.

I know it's not the first time you have realized the need for a change. You've realized this many times before. However, something was holding you back. You either didn't find the right techniques to change or didn't have the courage to do it. That's okay. This book will equip

4

you with the right skills and motivation to change your life, skills that will work to your advantage rather than others taking advantage of you.

Every change, even a small one, seems tough in the beginning. That's because we are creatures of habit, and we like living inside our comfort zones. We might not be satisfied with where we are, but still haven't mustered the courage to make a change.

However, let's find you the courage to take your first step towards change. If you want a new and unique way of restarting your game and taking charge of your life, start here. It's the easiest first step, and it's worth it.

Know what you want, say what you want, and get what you want. It may sound as simple as that, but it CAN be. Learn "how" here.

This book comes with a FREE booklet on masterminding a winning routine to improve calmness and your level of confidence everyday. Instructions on how you can download this booklet for free can be found at the bottom page of this book.

CHAPTER ONE

Assertiveness in a Diverse World

So, what's this 'assertiveness'? People commonly see assertiveness as being rude, domineering, or aggressive. However, the actuality is different.

Assertiveness is a social skill. It is a way of communication where you clearly and respectfully express your wants, needs, positions, and boundaries to others. This communication happens irrespective of your position or title. It's not being selfish, not being rude, but rather simply being firm and clear in your ways to communicate.

Being assertive is standing up for your rights calmly and positively without being aggressive or being too accepting even if something is 'wrong'.

Assertiveness in Psychology: Cognitive, Behavioral and Social Standpoint

An assertive person thinks, behaves, and speaks differently than others. He is calm, relaxed, and less anxious, even under stressful situations. That's natural because when you are clear about what you want and know how to communicate it to others, frustration and anxiety won't build up. You won't be fearful in your interpersonal interactions, and can easily achieve your goals.

On the other hand, people who lack assertive skills are more neutral and anxious. They fear the outcome of expressing their thoughts. What will others think of them? What if they lose people's approval? In short, non-assertive people are controlled by others and lack control over themselves.

Assertive people are firm without being rude. They equally regard other's opinions, thoughts, and wishes, as well as their own. They always react towards positive and negative emotions in a balanced way, without resorting to aggressiveness, shouting, or passivity. Assertive behavior has also been linked to lower levels of stress and depression.

Assertiveness also leads to transparency in your interactions. Assertive people know how to communicate their wishes and set boundaries, yet are not demanding, nor get furious when requests are not met. They confidently put their point of view in front of others and may even influence them to see their side. Yet, they respect others' opinions even if it differs from their own. They are open to constructive criticism.

So, considering assertiveness from unique aspects, what can you conclude?

It's clear that assertiveness is about controlling your own behavior, not others. With assertive behavior, you can acknowledge your thoughts and wishes honestly. You won't expect others to give in to your demands. You listen to others' feelings and opinions, respect them, but ultimately you choose to go along with them or not. Even if you go along with them, it's ultimately your decision. A decision that won't be made out of compulsion or helplessness. You won't be a people-pleaser with assertive behavior.

However, every great concept comes with a word of caution. Such is the case here. There's an optimal level of assertiveness to use, especially if you are a leader. Too much, or too little, and assertiveness will lose its desired effect.

Now, we'll explore in-depth the other communication styles besides assertiveness…

Assertiveness in Communication: The 4 Basic Styles of Communication

If I had to categorize people based on their style of communication, I'll place them in one of the following categories.

Passive communication

What do you think about these statements?

"I don't know about my rights."

"I can't stand up for my rights."

"People never consider my feelings."

They reflect a weak, depressed, even resentful personality. One who does not stand up for his own needs and feelings. This failure is a consequence of not identifying and expressing their needs and opinions.

And what happens when you don't express those ideas or needs?

You'll suffer silently while all that anger, hurt, and resentment builds up. Finally, it gets expressed as an emotional outburst, usually out of proportion to the triggering incident. You might feel embarrassed or guilty after the outburst but still, return to the passive style of communication.

Passive communicators rarely make eye contact while speaking and exhibit a slumped body posture.

Do you know how passive communication affects your life?

Passive communication can lead to:

- Anxiety and loss of control over one's life

- Hopelessness and depression

- Stress, resentment, and confusion

- Allowing others to take advantage of you or infringe on your rights

- Low self-esteem and confidence

- Poor decision-making

Aggressive communication

The exact opposite of the passive style is aggressive communication. An aggressive person expresses his feelings and advocates for his needs abusively. He is dominating, impulsive, and easily gets frustrated.

He humiliates others, criticizes, violates their rights, looks down upon them, and behaves rudely without giving heed to their feelings or opinions. Not only verbally, but their body language is also overbearing and aggressive.

It's only natural to think ill of such communicators who instill fear and hatred in others, and thus, typically lack true friends or a social circle.

You'll hear aggressive communicators saying things like, "I'm superior and I'm right" or "I'm the boss" or "I know better than you" or even "I'll get my way no matter what."

Passive-aggressive communication

Ever seen people muttering under their breath, maybe after a confrontation? They are the people who have a hard time speaking up, voicing their opinions face-to-face, or confronting issues directly. They'll appear to be passive on the surface but exhibit anger or aggressiveness in an indirect or subtle way.

Such people do not have the power to deal directly with their object of resentment. So, they'll show cooperation and acceptance on the surface, but will indirectly express their anger through taunts, sarcasm, and games.

The impacts of passive-aggressive communication can include:

- Feeling alienated from others
- Feeling powerless and stuck in life

- Incapability to address the real issues in life

Assertive communication

Assertive communication is a style where you clearly communicate your feelings and opinions and advocate for your rights without violating others' rights. In other words, you don't keep it all inside, or have emotional outbursts, nor do you fabricate things. You value yourself, your time, and your physical, emotional, and spiritual needs, as well as those of others around you.

Besides being a clear communicator, an assertive person is also a good listener. They establish eye contact when speaking to others, maintain a relaxed body posture, speak in a calm and clear tone, feel connected to others, and listen without interrupting.

Know why it's my favorite?

Because an assertive person:

- Feels competent and in control of his life
- Can address problems with confidence
- Creates a respectful environment for others to grow and mature
- Can take good care of himself, physically and mentally
- Can establish true, healthy, and long-lasting relationships

These are only a few of the statements I've heard from assertive communicators:

"We can communicate respectfully with each other."

"I am 100% responsible for my happiness."

"I always have a choice in life."

"I respect your feelings and rights."

However, the point to remember here is that we don't use a single style of communication in every interaction. The assertive style of communication is more likely to lead you into respectful and long-term relationships. So, it should be the preferred choice at most times.

Sometimes the situation may demand a passive or an aggressive style of communication. For example, the passive style would be a safer option if the situation is likely to escalate to violence. Similarly, if it's a question of your safety, aggressive communication may prevent the situation from getting worse.

Therefore, in every situation you must use your discretion to choose the best style of communication. If you feel your opinion might be better delivered by using another style of communication, choose that 'style' for that situation.

When you use one style of communication frequently, it gets embedded in your personality type. You become either a passive, an aggressive, or an assertive person.

What's the best way to identify these personalities? Let's explore some of the characteristics of each.

Characteristics of an Aggressive, Passive, and Assertive Person. Which one are you?

Each personality type has its own traits that make them different from others. Here's a synopsis of the personality traits of aggressive, passive, and assertive individuals. Which one do you fit in?

Characteristics of an aggressive person:

- He places his own needs over others'. He wants his desires fulfilled right away.

- Talks over other people

- No control over his emotions

- Blames other people for his failures

- Criticizes, humiliates, and talks ill about others

- Believes that a strong offense is the only way to defend himself

- Feels that speaking in a calm and friendly manner is a sign of weakness, and makes you prone to be taken advantage of. He thinks you have to be loud and strong to win.

Characteristics of a passive person:

- Sulky

- Withdrawn

- No eye contact

- Fearful to speak his mind lest he makes enemies

- Submissive because he hates conflict

14

- Appeasing to win people's approval

Characteristics of an assertive person:

- Calm, composed, and confident in a variety of situations

- Speaks clearly. His message is not exaggerated

- In control of self

- Can modulate himself when necessary

To summarize, the 3 C's of an assertive person are Confidence, Clarity, and Control. But how does an assertive person benefit in his life?

Why is assertiveness so important?

You'll get the answer shortly. Assertiveness leads to many benefits in your personal and professional life.

Assertiveness in your personal life helps to:

1. Be your own master. No matter what, you can hold on to your own and not be trampled by anyone.

2. Have your own way without being rude or creating a brawl, unlike aggressiveness, which is about forcing others into submission.

3. Better manage stress because of clarity in interactions. You know what to accept and when to say "no" thus setting clear boundaries for yourself and others.

4. Improve your self-esteem and confidence. Only an assertive individual has the confidence to speak up for himself.

5. Enhance your decision-making skills. Both passive and aggressive people make decisions based on emotions. On the contrary, assertive people tend to have a more neutral stance, keeping emotions in check and basing their decisions on facts.

Assertiveness in the workplace is important for:

1. Healthy and long-term relationships with your colleagues. When you are clear and transparent in your interactions in the workplace and speak politely with everyone, relationships are bound to be good.

2. Enhanced productivity of your team. Imagine a team leader who is aggressive and dominating toward his teammates. How would you feel to be on his team? Resentment and hatred, right? But if he was assertive? Valued your opinions and suggestions? The entire scenario would change. You would love working with him. The performance of the entire team would improve.

3. Better negotiation skills. You will never settle for less. You are also ready to modulate yourself where necessary.

4. A peaceful and friendly workplace where every individual, their feelings, and their opinions are respected. This will create a safe working environment for anyone and also leave room for new ways of thinking.

5. Achievement of your career goals. With all of these positive outcomes unfolding at the workplace, success will be yours!

Assertiveness in relationships

Success in relationships depends on honesty, clarity, and respect for each other. An assertive person will be well-versed in these behaviors, leading to successful relationships.

It's easy to see how important assertive behavior is; in personal life, work, and relationships.

Before proceeding to the techniques to create assertiveness in your life, it's time for some self-assessment.

Assertiveness self-scoring inventory

We have two essential components of assertiveness:

1. Express your wants, needs, and thoughts, even when it's difficult.

2. Respect what others want, need, and think, even when it's difficult.

To measure your proficiency in these two components, we have designed this Assertiveness Questionnaire to determine your level of assertive behavior in your day-to-day life.

Assertiveness Questionnaire

Please choose one response from below that best describes you. The responses vary on a scale from 1 (Not very like me) to 5 (Very like me).

Be honest! The information will be used to help you learn assertive behaviors in your work and relationships. There are no right or wrong answers. Just rate yourself on the scale from 1-5.

Key: 1 means very rare; 2 means sometimes; 3 mean usually; 4 means often; 5 means always

Questions→	Not very like me →→→ Very like me
	1　　2　　3　　4　　5
1. I stand up to people if they are doing something I'm not comfortable with	5
2. I speak up when someone doesn't respect my boundaries like "no cheating on me" or "I don't let friends borrow money"	4
3. It's often hard for me to say "No"	1
4. I express my opinions even if others disagree with them	1
5. After an argument, I often wish I would have said what	

was on my mind	5
6. I tend to go along with what my friends or colleagues want, rather than expressing my thoughts	1
7. I sometimes fear asking questions to avoid sounding stupid	1
8. I bottle up my feelings rather than talking about them	1
9. If I disagree with my boss, I talk to him or her	5
10. If a person has borrowed money and is overdue in returning it, I'll talk to the person about it	5
11. I'm usually able to tell people how I'm feeling	1
12. If I don't like the way someone is treated, I speak up about it	5

13. I speak up about things I really care about	5
14. I am careful to avoid hurting others' feelings, even if they have done wrong to me	5
15. I have a hard time controlling my emotions when I disagree with someone	1
16. I avoid attacking others' intelligence when I disagree with their ideas	5
17. I listen to others' opinions, even if I disagree with them	5
18. In disagreements, I make sure to understand the other person's point of view	3
19. During discussions, I communicate, and I am listening through body language	5
20. Even in an argument, I don't interrupt the other person	3

How to interpret the results

When you complete the questionnaire, you'll be tempted to add up your score. However, the total score has no meaning. Assertiveness must be assessed in terms of the person and the situation.

To analyze your responses to the Assertiveness Questionnaire, follow these steps:

1. Look at your responses to questions 1, 2, 4, 9, 10, 11, 12, 13, 14, 16, 17, 18, 19, and 20. These questions are oriented towards assertive behavior. Do your responses to these questions tell you that you always speak up for yourself or others'?

2. Look at your answers to questions 3, 5, 6, 7, and 8 which are oriented towards passive behavior. Do your answers reflect you are more submissive and let others take control over you?

3. Look at your answer to question 15 which suggests you push others around you more than you realize.

Chapter Summary

- There are 4 styles of communication - passive, aggressive, passive-aggressive, and assertive. Assertiveness is the most important and beneficial style of communication. Remember the benefits it pays you in personal, professional, and social life.

- There's an optimal level of assertiveness to use. Too much or too little, and you'll lose effectiveness.

- Did you complete the questionnaire to determine your style of communication? What's your level of assertiveness? Low or

21

high? Why do you want to learn and improve your assertiveness?

Answer these questions before you move on to the next chapter.

In the next chapter you will learn:

- Why some people can't be assertive.

- The major barriers to the practice of assertiveness.

- How you see yourself and how others see you, and which one matters.

- Skills to build a positive self-image.

CHAPTER TWO

Self-Discovery: Regaining Control of your Life

I'm sure some of you scored lower than you would have liked on your assertiveness self-assessment. That's okay! Most of us have been brought up that way, to see assertiveness as unimportant. Even if it were, we often lack the courage to use it.

Why? Why can't some of us be assertive? After all, we have the right to express our feelings, opinions, and beliefs. Yet still, we don't do it.

Who we are and why some of us are not assertive?

Each one of us is endowed with basic human rights that must be respected and upheld. These include:

- The right to express feelings, opinions, values, and beliefs

- The right to change one's mind

- The right to make decisions for ourselves

- The right to refuse if you don't know or understand something

- The right to say "no" without feeling guilty

- The right to be non-assertive

- The right to personal freedom

- The right to privacy

When you respond passively, you neglect or ignore others' rights, and allow others to infringe on them. In contrast, aggressive behavior abuses these rights of others. Assertiveness is the best way to balance upholding your rights as well as respecting those of others.

But assertiveness doesn't come easily to everyone, because of the following reasons:

Low self-esteem and confidence

When you feel poorly about yourself, you deal with people passively. That's because you believe that others' opinions and feelings are more important than your own.

Consequently, you give others the ability to make you feel lower and further lose confidence in yourself. This vicious cycle continues to reinforce low self-esteem and low self-worth.

Low-status work and gender roles

Low profile jobs (such as clerks, sweepers, etc.) and women are usually associated with non-assertive behavior. These people are placed under tremendous pressure to conform to their roles that often demand passiveness. Imagine a clerk who is less likely to be assertive to his boss than his co-workers or subordinates.

Past experiences

If you have been taught to behave in a non-assertive way, either by parents, role models or past experiences, it's difficult to change your ways and begin to behave assertively.

Stress and anxiety

When under stress, you often feel a loss of control over your life situations. Stress and anxiety usually result in the expression of thoughts and feelings in a passive or aggressive manner. This further increases your stress and the stress of those around you.

Personality traits

Some people are born with personality traits that are more passive or more aggressive. There's little they can do to change themselves. However, anyone can learn to be more assertive, while remaining true to the personality they were born with.

Unawareness of rights or wants

When you don't know what your rights are, or what you even want in the first place, you'll definitely find it difficult to exhibit assertive behavior.

Can you spot what's stopping you?

In the previous section, I listed the most common barriers that stop people from being assertive. Can you spot what's stopping you? Additionally, there are some individual needs and behaviors that pose a threat to the practice of assertiveness.

Here are some examples of such behaviors:

Desire to be loved at all costs

Every human being wants love and affection. However, in the workplace, this desire can quickly turn into a kind of dependency. Rather than being assertive and exercising your rights, you behave to please others and gain their approval.

Being kind to everyone

Being kind is good, but if it exceeds the threshold, it makes you too sensitive to the opinions of others. This can cause you to lose your independence. Also, people may start taking you for granted.

Intolerance to disagreements

Trying to convince others of your opinion at all costs is impulsive. Give others the freedom and the right to disagree. Staying detached from your opinion and giving others a chance to speak usually leads to progress, and even breakthroughs.

Seeking to control all situations

Humans are powerful beings, yet, we can't control everything and every situation. Nor can we control other people's behavior or way of thinking. But, when you try to do so, you end up being aggressive and forceful over others.

Obsession with perfectionism

Imagine a boss who wants everything to be perfect. He can't tolerate a single mistake from his employees. If that's his obsession with perfectionism, what will the workplace be like?

That's what happens when you seek perfectionism in every single task. You behave aggressively, not assertively. As a result, you push people away from you rather than establishing good relationships.

Trying to gain sympathy by overworking

When you overwork to show off or get sympathy from others, you don't challenge your limits, rather, you are seeking approval from others.

Intolerance to failure

When you say, "I don't have the right to make mistakes," you forget that mistakes are a part of being human. One who has never made mistakes has done nothing at all.

Setting contradictory goals for yourself

Setting goals that contradict your values and needs (professional and personal), or taking up responsibilities while hoping to avoid any conflicts, is preparing yourself for disappointment. It's more useful to set realistic and relevant goals for yourself and plan the steps you need to take to achieve them.

After analyzing all the barriers to assertiveness, one thing is absolutely clear. Everything comes down to what others will think of you. You fear losing others' approval and appreciation or want to control them lest they might think you are incompetent.

But do you correctly judge what others think of you? Let's find out in the next section.

Metaperceptions – how you see yourself and how others see you

If you say "I don't care what others think of me" you are only fooling yourself. Because ultimately, as humans, we all want to fit in with the social universe. The feeling of exclusion or rejection by a group leaves us anxious, irritated, and depressed.

To fit in socially, we need to connect with others. And to make good social connections, it helps to understand what others think of us and modify our behavior accordingly.

Knowing and perceiving what others think of you is called "metaperception." In other words, metaperceptions are how you feel about how others feel about you. Often these metaperceptions revolve around our perception of self – what we think about ourselves.

Mark Leary, a psychology professor at Wake Forest University in North Carolina says, "You filter the cues you get from others through your self-concept." This self-concept is fundamentally shaped by your mother. The way your mother responded to your first cries and gestures influences how you expect to be seen by others. Children with unresponsive mothers behave in ways that make people want to keep their distance, whereas those with responsive mothers are more confident and connect well with peers.

Though the self-concepts forged in childhood don't always carry on to adulthood, if they do, it takes a bit to change them, specifically the negative self-concepts. William Swann, a psychology professor at the University of Texas, conducted research that shows people with

28

negative self-concepts drive others to think negatively of them, especially if they suspect that others like them.

You all have a fairly stable view of yourself, but it's not always easy to determine what others think about you. Therefore, your metaperceptions are often inaccurate. Why?

First, every person you meet will perceive you through their unique lens. For example, if a person generally criticizes everyone, he will do the same with you, even if you are genuine. Second, people are sometimes not direct in daily interactions. They might fake their expressions.

However, you can make your metaperceptions more accurate by following these steps:

Be curious to learn new things and open to new experiences in life. As you take up new challenges, you'll meet new people from whom you can gather clear data about how you are perceived by others.

Take care of how you present yourself to others. Have a sense of your voice, tone, clothes, and body language. This way you can help control the impression you give and make your self-perception more accurate.

Learn to regulate your emotions and gain an upper hand in knowing what others think of you. If you are overwhelmed by your feelings or can't express them at all, it becomes difficult to interpret how others feel about you.

On the other hand, prickly and hostile behavior, bursting into tears at the slightest provocation, and narcissism block accurate metaperception. Such behaviors encourage others to become guarded, or even lie to you.

If you are socially anxious, you block accurate metaperception. You fail to ask others about themselves and fail to put others at ease while interacting with you.

So, being accurate in your metaperceptions is crucial. It rewards you by giving knowledge about how others perceive you and helps you fare better socially.

Others judge you on two types of traits—visible and invisible. People notice your visible traits more than you yourself. On a scale of physical attractiveness, others will almost always rate you a point higher than you would rate yourself.

Talking about the "invisible" traits, they aren't entirely invisible— at least not to your close friends. They can easily make out when you are anxious or worried. Your negative traits might be "invisible" for most, but if someone knows you really well, they can recognize them, too.

However, no one wants others to perceive their negative traits. We don't even acknowledge them, despite being aware of their presence, and modify our behaviors in order to avoid their disclosure.

Here's where self-awareness works against you and you get stuck with what you are, and your negative traits. Another realm where self-awareness acts as a curse is by overanalyzing others' reactions to you and misinterpreting them.

Unpleasant emotions like embarrassment, shame, and envy are also felt through self-awareness. These emotions are meant to motivate us and cut down our potentially self-destructive behaviors. However, when you get overly concerned about what others think of you, it can stifle your spirit and constrict your behavior.

Do you really want to know how people see you?

Report cards and annual reviews can track your performance in school and at work. But finding a straightforward critique of your character is difficult unless someone blurts out something in a heated argument.

You can always ask a family member or a close friend to tell you honestly what they think of you, but the question is: Are you ready to listen to their perspective?

This is because we all want to hear good things about ourselves. We can't tolerate anything negative. It hurts our ego. It hurts our self-image. We might even land in conflict with our loved ones to protect our own perspectives.

But sometimes you really need accurate feedback, like when deciding about a job change or a marriage proposal. That's where you need to learn how to see things from others' perspectives.

Perspective matters! The importance of seeing another perspective

Depending on where you stand, the view of your room can look very different. If you stand on one side of the room and your partner stands on the opposite side, you both will describe the same room, yet your descriptions will be different, simply because you are looking at the room from two different sides.

Similarly, perspectives in subjective matters can vary. The same fact will have a different meaning for people with different viewpoints. Like how a single divorce case can be viewed quite differently by different advocates. And sometimes, two opinions may be entirely opposite, yet are still both valid.

However, conflict arises when you fail to understand other perspectives. What makes sense to one person may sound absurd to you because you can't see their point of view. You can't take in other people's perspectives if they differ from yours.

Why? Here's the kicker!

Reality is how things are. But, for any person, what they think and feel is the reality for them, given the circumstances. What they think and feel further drives their actions.

Behavioral science research proves that we don't see things as they actually are. We filter them through our self-concept. Our personality and the way we are affected by the situations build up the way we see things. We interpret them according to what we believe is true about ourselves, about others, and our past experiences. All this builds our perspective about self and others which, once formed, is difficult to change. This tendency in humans is called confirmation bias. We see what we want to see, and thus, interpret information in a way that confirms our perspective.

That's why it's hard to truly understand another's perspective that is different than ours.

So even if a decision, event, or statement is the same, it can have different meanings for every individual or the group. And each of us may feel that we are right. However, that's the beginning of all misunderstandings, disagreements, and arguments.

If ONLY we could see things from another's perspective, we would have fewer conflicts and more productive conversations to combative issues. All the more, we would be more cautious with our words and actions in difficult situations to avoid making them worse.

For example, Theresa May's failure to get her Brexit deal through the House of Commons three times has stretched the Brexit drama far longer than most British people expected.

On such issues, can you keep your own perspective at bay, and try to see things from the other side?

The day you do so, you may find your own perspective not as accurate, or not the only "right" way. It's not that your perspective is wrong or you shouldn't stick to it for good reasons, but now, you better understand the other perspective.

Mistaking a perspective

However, there's a catch when trying to see things from another's perspective. You must avoid these two mistakes.

First, don't be overconfident that you have succeeded in interpreting a different viewpoint. Have you really seen it the way he thought/wanted? Are you sure you are not mistaken?

Research shows that when you infer the thoughts and feelings of a person by observing his face or the way he behaves, it's mostly inaccurate.

Next, avoid being easily pleased by the other person's perspective, and base your argument over it. Understanding another person's perspective doesn't mean you can't question it politely. When you base the perspective on wrong assumptions, you often make a misleading conclusion and miss the real issues.

For example, in the case of the Brexit deal, one may suspect that the leader is corrupt or faulty. If this speculation is accepted without raising a brow, the disagreements would eventually result in false judgments without addressing the actual problem.

How to take other perspectives in the right way

While taking another person's perspective into consideration, it's crucial to follow these three habits.

First, consider each perspective that differs from yours. Honestly include each of them. While comparing the different perspectives, you may come across some similarities. Plus, you may see how different perspectives can compensate for each other's strengths and weaknesses, and you may walk away with a new and better perspective.

Inclusivity also plays an important role when disagreements between perspectives are based on strong values and principles. If you pursue your own perspective driven by one of these values or principles, could it be that others are also motivated by some of these values and principles that are dear to you? So, consider the values or principles that back up a specific perspective, and how relevant they are.

Secondly, interact with people. You can't just imagine what the person is going through unless you have a conversation with him. You must interact with the person, ask questions, and listen to what he feels, his concerns, and ultimately his perspectives. When you are involved in such interactions, everyone is more likely to express their true feelings rather than simply saying the things that others want them to. This results in a better understanding of others' feelings, worries, and positions. Over time, such quality interactions also build trust and social collaborations.

Finally, strike a balance between your individuality and other's perspective. You must empathize with them, including their emotions and subjectivity, but also don't get carried away by them. Stay slightly detached so you can properly evaluate the situations and perspectives. Detachment doesn't mean to become feelingless, but to resolve the issue without getting entangled. In terms of opinions, detachment means you don't necessarily agree with others each time, but you always understand their perspective.

If you can be more considerate, interactive, and detached to manage arguments or disagreements, many differences will disappear. New pathways will open up that lead you towards common goals.

If you learn to appreciate another's perspective and use it appropriately, you can prevent misunderstandings, enable productive conversations, and achieve your common goals.

So ultimately what matters: How you see yourself or how others see you?

If you have followed me until here, it won't be difficult for you to answer that. It's legitimate to conclude that both have their value. Neither can be left out for the other. However, you should take everything with a detached mindset.

If you collect other's perspectives about yourself to improve your self-image or be a better version of yourself, it plays a positive impact on your life. Otherwise, if you get bowed down by other's viewpoints, it stifles your own character.

I'll talk more about building a positive self-image in the next section.

Building positive self-image

Self-image is how you see yourself, your personality traits, abilities, and what you believe others think of you. If you feel good about yourself, and recognize your strengths while being realistic about your shortcomings, then you have a positive self-image. Conversely, if you don't feel good about yourself, and focus on your faults and weaknesses while exaggerating your failures, you have a negative self-image.

You assess yourself both objectively and subjectively. Objective assessment is not influenced by personal feelings and represents facts such as your height, weight, hair color, IQ, etc. Subjective assessment includes traits such as care, affection, generosity, humor, patience, etc., and is influenced by your personal feelings. Since self-image is a collective representation of your self-assessment, it ultimately becomes more subjective than objective. People are generally more critical about themselves, and place a greater emphasis on their flaws rather than their goodness. Therefore, their self-image becomes biased.

A person's self-image is more or less resistant to change. However, it gets influenced by one's life experiences and interactions with others. Life experiences, both positive and negative, and interactions with family members, peers, and friends play significant roles in shaping self-image. For example, if you fail at a task and the people surrounding you also criticize and reject you, you may develop a negative self-image. Contrary to this, if your family and friends are supportive, they'll reinforce your positive attributes and help in developing your positive self-image.

As your experiences and relationships affect your self-image, so does self-image shape your experiences and relationships. If you have a positive self-image, you'll have a generally optimistic attitude. When you interact with others with such an attitude, they'll be uplifting and rewarding, thus contributing to a constructive relationship. These constructive relationships will further feed your positive self-image.

Your self-image is also closely connected with your self-esteem and self-confidence. Self-esteem is how you value yourself. Self-confidence is the trust in your knowledge, judgement, and abilities. Poor self-image will lead to low self-esteem and self-confidence. So, having a positive self-image is important as it affects your thinking, behavior, and how you relate to others around you. It enhances your physical, mental, emotional, and spiritual well-being, and gives you more confidence in your relationships. Even the people around you are influenced positively by your positive self-image.

However, the question is: How do you build a positive self-image?

Because, today, we all are the products of what others expect from us. We have often lost touch with what we "actually" are. Each one of us knows ourselves better than anyone else. We know what we think, what we feel, what we like and dislike, yet we still compare ourselves with others. This reflects our dissatisfaction with ourselves. And we are dissatisfied because we are far from being our true selves, which leaves us unhappy and emotionally drained.

So, follow these steps to uncover your real self:

Follow your passion. Be yourself by feeding your spirit, mind, and soul.

In modern times, money and wealth have become the metrics of a person's success. Consequently, you see young professionals taking up higher-paying jobs to make others feel proud of them.

The job might not be enjoyable for them, but since it pays well and earns them more respect, they prefer it. They pretend to be happy but may actually feel quite hopeless.

Sadly, people today often view each other in terms of their titles and salaries. These have become the determinants of one's self-worth. Instead, you should concentrate on just being yourself, which in turn will feed the mind, spirit, and soul. Cultivate your passion and find work you enjoy doing.

Never let your inner child die.

What can you best learn from a child? Being carefree!

Children don't care what others think about them because they're happy with themselves, with their lives. They are their own person because they haven't been modeled to fit into society and its funny norms. They enjoy running, playing, and jumping wherever they are and don't care what anybody thinks.

However, as you grow, you cast yourself as per other's expectations and lose touch with your inner child. Tickle your inner child again and become free by enjoying the moment and having fun.

Find your inner strengths.

Embrace yourself and your personality no matter how different you are from others. You could be an extrovert who's spontaneous or an introvert who's a bit awkward. Shed these labels that aren't important. You are what you feel and think. Get rid of all the pretending because you want to fit in. Just be yourself, and find your strengths. If other people are genuine, they'll accept the "real" you.

Tune into your feelings.

Acknowledge your feelings, good or bad. When you are in touch with your feelings, you understand more about yourself. Plus, it gives you the strength to deal with sadness, happiness, fear, or anger without getting stressed, and help you enjoy a peaceful state of mind.

Be more aware of your thoughts.

It's incalculable how many negative thoughts run through your mind every day. And after a period of time, these negative thoughts can start to turn into reality. Because that's the law of nature. Every thought manifests into a reality. So, you must take extra care of your thoughts and their quality. Regular meditation helps you become more aware of your thoughts and gives the power to change them. Then, throughout the day, continue to observe your thoughts. By becoming more aware of them, and changing those thoughts when needed, you'll focus more on your present.

Trust your intuitions.

It's always advisable to follow your intuition. It's one of the most essential parts of being you. As you begin trusting your intuition, you transform into your most authentic self, which is the "real" you.

You may believe that a wise decision is practical and serves more purpose, but this isn't always true. Practical decisions are made on what is thought to be right, and not what is felt to be right. When you make a decision by following your intuition, your soul will be satisfied.

Get out of your shell.

While learning to be yourself, you may feel tempted to do everything at once. You want to get rid of all the masks, pretensions, and become totally authentic overnight. However, it doesn't work that way. First, you should identify the ways you're socially inauthentic and then correct them one at a time. Get out of your shell gradually to be more authentic in your life. Start by setting small goals to change and work gradually and consistently to achieve them one by one. Small steps lead to a big change. You'll achieve your goals soon, and find yourself behaving entirely differently than before.

Calm down. Be assured that it's okay to be yourself.

Many people feel tense or anxious when trying to be themselves. If you are one of those, first, calm down, and assure yourself that it's perfectly alright to be "myself." The ONLY way to do this is through self-talk. Sit in silence for a few minutes, observe what's going on in your mind, and make it understood through inner dialog. Just like we would make a child understand, in an assuring and convincing way. Do the same with your mind now. You need to tell yourself that it's okay to be your real self. If others don't like it, that's their problem. This self-talk will relieve your tension and anxiety and help you interact better in social settings.

Deal with your anxiety

Go a step further and read some books on how to deal with anxiety. Your lack of positive self-image might be more than just a little lack of confidence. It could stem from some serious social anxiety. Taking steps to handle social anxiety will prove beneficial in discovering your true self.

Once you connect with your "real" self using these steps, I assure you that you'll start feeling good about yourself. You'll learn to accept and love yourself as you are. And when that happens, others also start accepting you as you are, too.

Case Study: The Power of Perspective and Positive Self-Image

John is excited to go out on his first date. He really likes the young woman he is going out with, so he is really keen to make a good impression and connect with her. However, over the course of their discussion on the date, he learns that she is motivated and driven by completely different values. She has very different tastes in almost everything. Now, what does John do to make a good impression?

He respects the woman's opinions and values, but also offers his own. Instead of blindly following her opinions on things, he isn't afraid to disagree with her openly, yet respectfully.

His positive self-image and high self-esteem allow him to stay true to his values and easily communicate with others, even when they don't agree. That's because John believes more in behaving authentically than focusing on getting his date to like him.

So, what do you think about yourself? Do you have a positive or a negative self-image for yourself? Let's find out with the next questionnaire.

Self-assessment for self-discovery

Yup! I am back again with yet another self-assessment activity for you. I promise it'll be fun and deliver real insight, something that is very critical in seeking to be the master of your life.

So, don your thinking caps and answer the following questions honestly:

1. What are your strengths?

    a. List 5 things you love about yourself.

    b. List 5 abilities, skills, or talents you have.

    c. List 5 life achievements or instances you "win" in your life.

    d. List 5 difficult situations you overcame.

    e. List 3 - 5 people who are your best supporters.

    f. List 3 - 5 people you have helped in some way.

    g. List 5 things you are grateful to have in your life.

2. What are your major barriers to assertiveness?

3. What are the areas you need to shift your perspective in order to change your life?

Chapter Summary

43

- Low self-esteem, low self-confidence, unawareness about one's rights, stress, and anxiety are the major barriers to the practice of assertiveness in daily life.

- Building a positive self-image and giving due consideration to others' perspectives (different) are the keys to use the assertive style of communication.

- Follow your passion, tune in to your feelings, be aware of your thoughts, find your inner strengths, trust your intuitions, and get out of your comfort zone to discover your real self and build a positive self-image.

In the next chapter you will learn:

- What is personal empowerment and how to achieve it?

- What does personal empowerment feel like?

- The relationship between assertiveness and empowerment.

- How to assert yourself positively.

CHAPTER THREE

Using Your Personal Power

As discussed in the last chapter, building a positive self-image allows you to be the master of your life. Positive self-image empowers you.

Why do we all want to feel empowered?

Because without empowerment people lack control over what they do. They lack confidence in themselves and their decisions, and thus, rely on others to make decisions for them – their spouse, colleague, children, or peers. They often feel dominated by their colleagues, friends, or family, or overwhelmed by the demands of their job. In contrast, empowered people are fully in charge of what they do, what they want in life, and how to achieve it.

What is personal empowerment?

"Empowerment" literally means "becoming powerful." That doesn't mean growing in strength like a Sumo wrestler or attaining the most influential position at your workplace. True empowerment requires you to set meaningful goals by identifying what you want in life and then taking action to achieve those goals, thus making a significant difference in this world.

Therefore, personal empowerment is to take control of your own life, and not allow others to control it for you. Also, be clear that "empowerment" is not the same as "entitlement." Entitled people believe that all the benefits and privileges should come to them automatically. On the other side, empowered people achieve success through hard work, reflection, and cooperation.

As easy as it sounds, the process of personal empowerment is complicated. To empower yourself, you need to develop your self-awareness, which helps you understand your strengths and weaknesses. Plus, you must be aware and understand your goals, how they differ from your current position, and what behaviors, values, or beliefs you need to change in order to achieve them. The degree of this change required varies from person to person.

But I did promise to make complex issues easier for you!

So, I have outlined an eight-step process for you to develop personal empowerment easily. Let's dive in to learn the process step-by-step.

Step 1: Identify a goal focused on power

This might be, for example, a housewife seeking financial independence from her spouse, or someone looking to have more influence over their teammates.

Step 2: Increase your knowledge

The next step is to understand more about the goal you have set. For example, if you don't want to be financially dependent on your partner, you need to understand the various ways to earn money by working from home. Also, open yourself up to different possibilities. The more open you are, the more creative you get, and the more possibilities appear for you to succeed in.

Step 3: Increase your self-efficacy

Before you take action to achieve your goal, you need to believe that you can achieve your goal. Having information about your goal is one thing. But you must also understand your strengths and weaknesses. That's what self-awareness is all about. It also includes being aware of your values and beliefs, and their critical examination to ensure they are fully valid. This will help you assess where you are most likely to achieve.

Step 4: Work on your skills and competence

You may need to enhance your skills to become more influential. These skills can be acquired through experience, education, training, or practice. As you start interacting with more and more people, and try to influence them, you will rapidly learn what works, and further develop your skills.

Step 5: Act and keep taking action

The road to personal empowerment won't be smooth. You will encounter bumps along the way. However, instead of getting "knocked back" by the first obstacle you encounter, you should maintain the resilience and persistence to keep moving and seek other ways to achieve your goals.

Step 6: Run your own race

Don't be bowed down by the competition. Don't worry if the grass seems greener on the other side. It doesn't equate to your failure. Focus on your grass, on the opportunity that is in front of you.

If you worry about the competition, what others are and are not doing, then you'll lose track of the importance of what you're doing. Empowerment has nothing to do with competition, it has everything to do with what you contribute to the world.

Step 7: Assess your impact

Empowerment is also about changing the impact you have on others and your life situations. Therefore, it's important to also assess your impact. At first, you may not see huge changes, but even small changes count as your success.

Step 8: Expand your network

Empowerment comes from collaboration, not competition. Success is never a one-man job. One of the smartest ways to develop personal empowerment is to network. Build a network of people who have strengths to fill in your limitations. In collaborative environments, success is shared, and each person empowers the other.

Competition divides us, and may sometimes lead to jealousy or anger, none of which will help you build long-term relationships or be more successful.

How does language affect your personal empowerment?

The way you express yourself, both verbally and non-verbally, to others can empower you as well as the people with whom you communicate. For example, using a positive and active language like "I will" and "I can" is empowering whereas the opposite implies passivity, lack of control, and lack of responsibility for your actions.

While introducing yourself to others, use your own words to describe yourself, and not how others define you. Otherwise, people may persuade you to conform to their demands.

Never criticize a person to their face. If criticism is absolutely necessary, exercise it with extreme caution. Use positive and supporting words and phrases to offer criticism in a constructive way. For example, if your teammate is always late to work but is a very hard worker, praise his hard work. Tell him if he can work so hard, he can also be punctual. Your words will work like magic. They'll empower him to at least try to be on time.

That's how your language can play a significant role in your personal empowerment and those of others. Now, let's see what personal empowerment feels like by walking through an example.

A Case Study: What does personal empowerment feel like?

Amara and Shira are best friends. They both divorced their husbands within one year of marriage. They sincerely tried to make their marriages work but didn't succeed. Nor did they receive the required alimony from their husbands.

Do they feel empowered?

In Amara's case, she actually is. Though she was sad for a few days after the divorce, she decided to move on. She didn't want to be stuck. She took up a job of her liking, made new friends, and is now preparing for her second marriage.

Shira, on the other hand, is depressed, frustrated, and full of tears. She is convinced that her life has come to a standstill since the divorce. Every day she keeps blaming her husband and reiterating how he did not treat her well. She wants to work, she wants to meet new people, but she is afraid to be rejected because of her divorce.

Amara knew what she wanted from her life. So, she made a decision and acted on it. Shira, in contrast, feels powerless to change her situation, so she doesn't even try. She lacks confidence and empowerment to achieve what she wants. This becomes a vicious cycle. Because of the lack of empowerment, she doesn't try. And because she doesn't try, she doesn't achieve to feel empowered.

However, empowerment doesn't only come from achieving. You must speak up and take a stand for yourself to feel empowered. In other words, you must be assertive in order to feel empowered.

Let's explore the relationship between assertiveness and empowerment in the next section.

Assertiveness and empowerment

Consider the following situation:

Nancy works in the HR department of a company. She's a young, beautiful, married woman. Her company has organized an office trip to Goa. All her colleagues are going except her. That's because her husband feels she can't go on a trip without him. He thinks she can't take care of herself without him.

So, Nancy suppresses her excitement for the trip and goes along with the situation. A few months later, Nancy's boss throws a lavish party at his home, inviting her and her husband. But again, her husband refuses to go to the party, giving some lame excuse and doesn't allow Nancy to go, either.

Time and again Nancy has had to suppress her feelings because of her husband.

Does that sound like your story?

Well, that's because Nancy and you choose to suffer in silence rather than expressing your feelings. You behave passively, lest you hurt others' feelings. This might seem to be using your powers for good, not hurting others' feelings, but that's an illusion.

Being passive makes you feel like a victim, one who is trapped in their life situation and can't get out of it without the help of others. Playing a victim will never let you feel empowered. You'll always be at the mercy of others.

Contrastingly, Nancy could have become aggressive, by shouting or yelling at her husband. Aggressiveness usually develops out of a sense of entitlement and is another common way for people to assume a sense of power, or to feel powerful. Such people believe that aggressiveness is the justified way to deal with situations like these, by controlling others. However, the power of aggressiveness is unhealthy and can severely damage your relationships. If it becomes your regular method of gaining control over situations, it will alienate you from others and may even create anxiety in people involved.

Besides the passive and aggressive approaches towards controlling situations, some people take the passive-aggressive approach. It's a deadly combination of two unhealthy approaches. When two people are in a relationship, this passive-aggressive behavior makes things much more complicated.

In Nancy's case, she may conform to her husband's demands on the surface but punish him silently, for example, by not cooking good food for him. A person with passive-aggressive behavior feels they are powerful, but, in reality, they lose their integrity and reduce any possibilities of healthy empowerment.

Healthy empowerment and how assertiveness plays a role

So how do we differentiate healthy empowerment from unhealthy empowerment?

That's simple! Healthy empowerment doesn't allow people to act at the expense of others. A person with healthy empowerment knows how to navigate his life with confidence and purpose. If an empowered person does commit a mistake that hurts someone, he'll apologize and seek healthy ways for resolution, considering the other person's needs.

Additionally, an empowered person lets the other know if he feels tread upon or taken advantage of. Love and respect for self, and others, are the life mantra of an empowered (healthy) person.

When you feel empowered, you also feel liberated. You take responsibility for your actions, which are unaffected by how other people behave. Here are four tips to help you become more assertive and feel empowered in your life:

Be friendly, not accommodating

There's a difference between *being friendly* and *accommodating people.*

Friendly means taking care of your loved ones and helping them in times of need. On the other hand, you accommodate people when you care for them at the expense of yourself. You simply don't know when to say no. Consequently, you build up anger and resentment inside. You feel that people take undue advantage of your inability to say "no."

So, the choice is yours: whether to be friendly, or whether to be accommodating to people. When you choose "being friendly," you not only befriend others, you're also being friendly to yourself.

Understand that taking care of others' needs doesn't mean sacrificing your own. For example, if your friend asks you for financial help with something you can't, simply refuse or ask to be reimbursed. This way you won't feel like the victim of other people's demands.

Speak up, not out

When you don't know what assertiveness is, you picture someone who is overly harsh and demanding. However, assertiveness is about speaking up, not speaking out. Speaking out is getting angry when your needs are not met, or yelling and blaming others when they manipulate you.

Speaking up, on the other hand, is making people aware of your needs upfront. You don't shout at or blame others, rather you proactively set reasonable expectations and boundaries. Communicating with others what you need helps build healthy, strong relationships, as well as your self-esteem.

Define your boundaries

Boundaries are important, and it is equally important to keep them defined. Despite setting the boundaries, some people will try to cross them. Then what?

Keep your boundaries well-defined and reinforce them with those that try to cross them. Come what may never give in to the demands of those people. Otherwise, you'll invite them to walk over your boundaries again and again.

Let go of the selfish "friends"

You know who your selfish "friends" are! They're warm and complimenting but will interact with you only when you give something in return.

Can you call these individuals your "true" friends? Will they not trample your boundaries and expect you to give in to their demands?

If you worry about losing them, relax! You don't have to tell them that things aren't working out. They'll automatically leave you when they realize you won't do anything for them anymore. Some may try to make you feel guilty but try not to listen. Don't fret over losing selfish friends. It's good that they leave your life. You deserve the true ones.

Thus, the lack of empowerment makes you feel helpless. Your life is in the hands of others. They can make you dance like a puppet on their whims and fancies. This creates anxiety and resentment.

However, becoming more assertive puts the power and control back in your hands.

How to assert yourself positively

There's a fine line between being assertive and being aggressive. And if you seek to feel empowered, to feel more in control of your life, and to lead a happy, positive, and fulfilled life, you need to be assertive.

Yet, the question remains! How do you assert yourself positively?

People generally consider themselves as assertive, but in reality, they've had situations where they let things just slide by. They didn't stand up for themselves. Result? Anger, resentment, frustration, and guilt get bottled up.

Some people, when they confront a difficult situation, feel that it's easier to run away rather than facing it head-on. That's because they lack the inner power; the empowerment we've been talking about.

However, it's much more effective to be a strong and mighty lion than a timid mouse, running away from danger. It's time to take a closer look at assertiveness and learn the steps to be a "lion" in your life.

But, why only the lion? Because the lion symbolizes strength and power, which you ultimately want and will help you achieve your life goals.

Here are the seven easy steps for asserting yourself positively:

Create an image of strength in your mind

Consider the example of the lion I gave above. Hold that image of yourself as a lion in your mind, and relive it when faced with a situation where you need to assert yourself. If a lion doesn't seem feasible to you, choose whatever image conveys strength and power to you. Come back to it when you need an assertive boost. Creating and commemorating the image of strength in your mind keeps you alert on being assertive. It also gives you the confidence that you can assert yourself positively.

Believe in yourself and your values

The first step to being assertive is to believe in yourself and what's important to you. Without this self-awareness or a firm sense of self, it will be difficult to stand up for yourself and be assertive when necessary.

You have to know who you truly are, and what you believe to be a truly assertive person. Start working on developing your self-awareness today. Find your strengths to make the most of the situations where you need to stick to your beliefs.

Understand your own boundaries

You can't be assertive unless you know where your boundaries lie, and when someone crosses them. It's essential to define and communicate to others what makes you uncomfortable.

You have to be clear as to what you'll tolerate and what you won't. But before communicating this to others, you must be clear with yourself, otherwise, you won't know when a line has been crossed.

Understand your needs and your purpose of assertiveness

What is that you want to achieve by asserting yourself?

It might be to stop another person's unpleasant behavior or to reach a specific goal. You must know this: what you want and what purpose you wish to fulfill by asserting yourself positively. That's because your purpose might get lost in the heat of the moment. So, make sure you remember your values when trying to determine your goal.

Respect others (and yourself)

We've established that there is a fine line between being assertive and being aggressive. You can be assertive without humiliating others. You can be assertive without putting others (and yourself) in a vulnerable or uncomfortable position.

How? Be respectful. You can behave with respect and kindness even when being assertive. Put yourself in their shoes, and think about how you would like to be treated. Assert yourself while keeping this in mind. Being respectful of others will also make you maintain your integrity and conduct yourself in a manner that you can be proud of.

Express expectations clearly

To be assertive in any situation, it is imperative that you clearly express what you expect from others. Because if you are not clear about what you want, it will be very hard for others to give what you want.

While expressing your expectations, use clear and direct language. Avoid using vague terms or words that may be confusing. It might feel hard to be direct sometimes, but if you're clear about what you want, you are more likely to get what you want.

Remember: no one is omniscient and can read your mind or know what you want. You have to express it clearly.

Practice assertiveness often

You all have heard this before: practice makes perfect!

So, if you want to improve your assertiveness skills, you have to practice them often. That doesn't mean insisting on getting your way all the time, but rather realizing your needs and valuing them just as much as those of others.

Think of the situations where you could have been assertive, but weren't. Think about if similar (or worse) situations arise in the future, how you could positively assert yourself. Rehearse it! Practice it as much as you can.

Rebuilding your life from a foundation of respect

One question that still pervades your mind: how do I respect my own needs and that of others at the same time? Don't I have to compromise my own needs, in order to create peaceful relationships? Isn't it easier to remain quiet than expressing my needs?

Short answer: NO.

You don't have to be a people pleaser to create better relationships. Or, meet this need by silencing your self-expression. This leads you to be passive and bottle up anger and resentment. The key is to refocus on your needs and respect them. This is called self-respect; it is your ability to see the "self" having the same basic rights and dignity as others.

In the last three centuries, the world has witnessed an immense increase in people's civil rights. The Declaration of Human Rights, signed by most countries, ensures equal dignity and basic rights to people irrespective of their social class, gender, religion, etc.

However, it's surprising that people still do not claim their rights or assert themselves, though they possess these rights. Like people who are mobbed or bullied and silence themselves instead of protesting against injustice. Some people accept less pay for their work even if their performance is the same as others.

And why does this happen? Research shows that when people perceive themselves as equal to others, they expect equal treatment. But, when they don't, they consider unequal treatment as just and protest as inappropriate.

59

Thus, to claim one's rights or behave assertively, one must view oneself as equal to others. In other words, they must have a good amount of self-respect.

But, what does it mean to perceive yourself as equal to others? How do you respect your own needs and that of others at the same time?

Let's understand this with a few examples.

Suppose you're at a restaurant and unhappy with the service. A passive response would be to stay quiet. An aggressive response would be to yell at the server. An assertive response would be to kindly let the server know what you'd want. Here, you're speaking up for your needs while also respecting the server.

Let's see another one.

Your employee is a bit lazy and doesn't complete their assignment on time. Instead of shouting and scolding, an assertive response would be to set clear expectations with your employee.

We can respect others' needs and our own by making "requests" rather than "demands." Demands don't consider the other person's needs or opinions and usually backfire. Requests, on the other hand, consider the needs of both parties in question. People are more likely to respond to requests as they feel connected and have a choice to agree or not.

If you can't hear a "no," then it's a demand. If you are open to finding strategies that work for both of you, it's a request. Requests increase the possibility of what the other person is willing to do.

So respecting others' needs doesn't mean compromising your own, or remaining silent, or letting others take advantage of you, or becoming a people pleaser. Rather, it is about compassionately and acknowledging others' needs and making requests (not demands) to meet your needs. After all, you deserve to have a voice.

Chapter Summary

- Personal empowerment and developing self-respect are the necessary requirements to develop assertive behavior.

- Set a powerful goal for yourself, acquire knowledge, work on your skills and competence, and keep working to achieve your goals. This will help you feel empowered from within.

- Believe in yourself and your values, understand your needs, your boundaries, and set clear expectations with others to assert yourself positively and develop your self-respect.

- You deserve to have a voice. Compassionately and clearly acknowledge others' needs and make requests (not demands) to meet your own.

- I would appreciate it if you could answer the questions below before we get into the nitty-gritty of developing assertive behavior.

1. Do you view yourself as equal to others? Why or why not?

2. List any 3 situations in your life where you feel you could have been assertive but didn't.

3. What are the areas you feel you lack empowerment? How can you feel empowered in these aspects of your life?

In the next chapter you will learn:

- Why assertiveness is a learned skill

- Three keys for assertive behavior

- The various categories of assertive behavior

- How to handle criticism assertively

- How to speak up for yourself

CHAPTER FOUR

Getting Started: Developing the Assertive Behavior

Now you are familiar with what assertiveness is and what qualities you need to develop assertive behavior in yourself. The real (and the fun part!) starts now - how to develop assertive behavior.

Assertiveness is a learned skill

Assertiveness is not only a style of communication, but a characteristic mode of behavior that involves expressing your thoughts, feelings, beliefs, and opinions openly, without violating the rights of others.

And any mode of behavior can be learned through consistent practice. However, the practice of assertive behavior is associated with the following dos and don'ts:

Dos of assertive behavior

1. Expressing your needs clearly and directly

2. Expressing your ideas without feeling guilty

3. Standing up for what you believe even though others may not agree

4. Knowing your rights and how to get them

5. Effective communication

6. Conveying your feelings to others with confidence

7. Self-reliance and independence

8. Persisting until your needs are met

9. Analyzing a problem and pinpointing the area of responsibility before taking an action

10. Having a positive attitude at all times

11. Being strong when others are weak

12. Taking pride in your accomplishments

13. Having the courage to dream and developing the skills to turn them into reality

Don'ts of assertive behavior:

1. Beating around the bush before expressing your needs

2. Feeling guilty or afraid to express your needs

3. Agreeing with others no matter how you feel

4. Ignorance about your rights

5. Ineffective communication

6. Begging for what is legitimately yours by law

7. Dependence on others

8. Giving up when you face problems

9. Giving in to defeat

10. Easily swayed by others

11. Uncomfortable about your accomplishments

12. Fear to dream

Practicing assertiveness is not a new concept. Many people and organizations have achieved their objectives through assertive techniques for decades. Here are a few examples of individuals who have "won" and reached their goals by being assertive:

- Susan B. Anthony, whose persistence in the long struggle for female suffrage won American women the right to vote in 1919.

- Mohandas K. Gandhi's determination freed India and inspired subjugated people all over the world to emulate his nonviolent methods to gain freedom.

- Carol Mosely Braun, who shook up Illinois politicians when she defeated the "undefeatable" Alan Dixon in the Illinois Democratic primary for U.S. Senate.

- Jane Bryne (former Chicago mayor), whose outspoken assertiveness got her fired from her job in City Hall, but a year later, she was elected as the head of the City Hall.

- Patrick Henry. His assertive quote, "Give me liberty or give me death" became the rallying cry of the American Revolution.

- Jesse Jackson's positive attitude overcame discrimination and poverty to become a powerful national leader.

- Joan of Arc, whose courageous assertiveness inspired a defeated French army to victory.

The people who stand out as doers, movers, and achievers are all assertive people, though their specific styles may differ.

Indeed, we are all born with an innate temperament to assert ourselves. But, as we grow up and socialize, it may either reinforce our innate tendencies or curtail them. The responses we receive from our family, peers, co-workers, and authority figures as children play a significant role in shaping our innate tendencies.

For example, if your family dealt with conflicts by yelling or arguing, you'll learn to deal with conflicts in the same way. On the other hand, if your family or peers believe in expressing your thoughts while respecting those of others, you'll likely develop the same habits.

When you grow up as an assertive individual, you tend to be emotionally balanced and have better health outcomes. However, being assertive doesn't guarantee that you'll ALWAYS get what you want. Sometimes you will, sometimes you won't, and sometimes you'll agree upon mutually satisfactory action.

I know what you must be thinking. You haven't grown up as an assertive person. People around you always taught you to put others' needs before your own, to please others before yourself. And now you find it hard to assert yourself. Relax! As I said, assertiveness is a skill and it can be learned at any stage of your life. Even now! So, let's dive in to learn more about how to develop assertive behavior.

We have already gone over the difference between passive, aggressive, and assertive styles of communication. Now, let's inspect these three different styles.

Behaving *aggressively*, even if you are right, communicates to others, "What I want is more important than what you want." You put others' needs at stake, in fact, outwardly disrespecting them. As a result, the recipients of your aggression feel resistant and often counterattack in anger. This can lead to conflicts, arguments, stress, and even hatred in relationships.

Being *passive* is not any better. It's living a lifestyle devoid of the word "no," which is like driving a car without brakes. When you say "no" you set appropriate limits to what you accept and what you don't. Without these limits, your life will be out of control and full of stress, anger, and resentment. Saying no at the right time and for the right reason is healthy, proper, and good. That's what assertiveness is all about!

Assertive behavior is the positive and controlled expression of your legitimate needs. It's a healthy way to communicate where you maintain your self-respect and also earn respect from others.

It's a healthy way to deny something with dignity. Being assertive allows you to get what you need without hurting others. It's a perfect balance between aggressive and passive behaviors.

Assertive behavior allows you to lead a life of peace, respect, and cooperation. An assertive person advocates for himself, but in a respectful and determined way, yet, acknowledging the feelings and rights of others.

The messages with the use of "I" typically reflect assertive behavior.

For example:

- I can't make it to the meeting today.

- I would appreciate it if you can help me with this.

- I am really not in the mood to go to the party.

- I am sorry, I already explained the consequences for being late to the office today, and now you have to face them.

Contrary to what many believe, assertive behavior evokes respect from others, whereas the other styles do not.

When you behave assertively, people know that "you mean what you say" and it's not an exaggeration or bluffing. Your "yes" means "yes" and your "no" means "no." Such clear communication is beneficial for all parties involved and builds trust and cooperation.

People feel more comfortable with those who are transparent and open about their thoughts and feelings. An assertive style of communication includes how you think, speak, and conduct yourself.

Behaving assertively also reduces your stress levels. Passivity is synonymous with the feeling of powerlessness and being overwhelmed.

Aggressiveness often encounters resistance and counterattacks. These are extremely stressful.

In contrast, an assertive individual takes a balanced, calm, yet determined approach to get what he or she needs. Assertive behavior is the least stressful path.

Let's understand assertiveness with a true story.

Julie appreciates when her husband Jack refuses to help her with household chores. She knows when he can't or doesn't want to do something. Plus, she knows that when he does say "yes" to something, he actually means it, and will follow through.

Jack's assertive behavior towards Julie is an act of respect and honesty. If Julie doesn't agree with Jack about something, she knows she can, in turn, respectfully disagree with him. So together, they can resolve their issues, and arrive at a mutually agreed-upon plan of action.

The three keys of assertive behavior

The three keys of assertive behavior can be related to a three-legged chair. You can sit on a three-legged chair without worrying about falling, but not on a two-legged chair. Assertive behavior is also characterized as having three legs.

The three basic components of assertive behavior are:

1. **Know what you want**. Be clear as to what it is you want.

2. **Say what you want**. Communicate your intentions, needs, and desires to others clearly without using any vague or confusing language.

3. **Get what you want**. With respectful, determined, and controlled means of communication, increase the likelihood of achieving your reasonable and legitimate goals.

Categories of assertive behavior

Before you even open your mouth, your body language says a lot about you. It announces to others if you are confident about yourself or not.

Body language that shows confidence:

- Standing up straight and making eye contact when speaking with others

- Sitting in a relaxed, but professional manner

- Taking an initiative to greet others at a meeting and in opening the conversation

- Confidently sit next to the most powerful person in the room

- Not waiting for permission to speak before speaking up

- Organized in work and has the needed information at their fingertips

- Dressing appropriately

- Courteous and pleasant during discussions

Body language that shows a lack of confidence:

- Slumped posture when standing

- Afraid to look at people when talking to them

- Sitting down as though sitting on eggshells, too self-conscious to move

- Afraid to take the initiative in greeting people and waits for others to give permission to say "hello"

- Sitting inconspicuously

- Afraid to speak unless spoken to and given specific permission to speak

- Seldom carrying information or materials to meetings

- Under or overdressed for a picnic or a party

- Getting unpleasant, argumentative or rude when expressing a viewpoint

An assertive person communicates with confidence, both in body language and verbally. There are three categories of assertive behavior:

Refusal assertiveness is saying "no" at the right time and in the right way. Saying "no" helps you establish healthy boundaries and allows others to know what they can expect from you. It also makes you feel empowered and maintains strong relationships.

A useful strategy to help you say "no" with ease is to gain clarity about the types of things that you wish to say "yes" to. Jot down your top three priorities (which might change over time) in a diary or notepad,

71

and always keep it handy. When someone asks you something, check to see if it aligns with your priorities. If yes, feel free to answer the inquiry affirmatively. If it is not in line with your objectives, say no.

Follow these steps to say no in the right way:

- State your position, like if you can't take up a task, "No, I can't."

- Explain your reason: Give a valid reason for your inability to take up a task, for example, if you are occupied with other important issues.

- Express your understanding for the other person.

If you don't have an immediate answer to someone's inquiry, ask him to give you a certain period to think over it and provide a deadline by which you'll answer. This keeps you accountable and ensures you value the relationship and yourself by providing a concrete reply in the desired time frame.

Expressive assertiveness is telling people how you feel. Expressing your feelings is an essential component of effective communication.

10 times where you must express yourself:
- When you love someone.

- When you feel strongly about something.

- When something bothers you.

- When you feel like you can't cope, speak up, and ask for help.

- When you disagree with someone.

72

- When you're not happy in a situation.

- When someone has done something great for you.

- When you have a question, always ask it.

- When you have an answer, always give it.

- When you have good news, always share it.

No doubt you must express your positive, as well as your negative feelings. However, gloomy feelings must be expressed with a word of caution. You must take ownership of those feelings rather than blaming others.

For example, if your friend arrives late for dinner, you might say, "You made me angry by arriving so late for dinner." Your friend might have arrived late, but they are not responsible for your reaction. Your feelings, in reality, are the result of your own expectations and hopes. If you express them in a way that puts the blame on others, it's more likely to meet a defensive response. The other person may not acknowledge your feelings, and then the issue remains unsolved.

If I were in your place, I would express my feelings as "I was so angry when you arrived late for dinner, because I had hoped to spend some quality time together."

See the difference? I took responsibility for my own feelings. When you clearly express your feelings without assigning blame and express why you feel that way, it enables the other person to understand and acknowledge your feelings.

Request assertiveness is to get the information, its clarification, and ask for what you want. When you lack the skill to make assertive requests, you make life unnecessarily hard for you and others. You may miss out on opportunities, take longer to complete things, or make them more complicated.

In contrast, when you learn to make requests assertively, you respect yourself and others. By asking directly, what you need, you say, "I have value" and "I value your help." So, it's essentially a compliment to the other person.

What stops you from making assertive requests?

See if any of these beliefs resonate with you:

- If someone denies my request, it means they don't like and/or respect me.

- Asking for help puts me under an obligation to them.

- Asking for help means I am weak OR other people will see me as weak.

- It's better to do it myself than risk rejection.

- I will annoy or upset others by asking for help.

- I don't want to be a burden/add to their stress/workload.

- I don't deserve to ask for help.

- I shouldn't have to ask; people should know I need help.

- Other people will help me only if I'm excited about it.

- People should help me as I'm more important or more stressed than they are.

These beliefs make it hard to ask for help. And even if you do, you'll likely encounter resistance. However, the point to remember is that these beliefs might be just your feelings. Just because you feel them doesn't make them true.

In addition, if you ask for help, you might get something done faster, more smoothly, or more easily. You might get a better job, learn something new, share your experiences, or get to know someone better. This will help you build better relationships and show people who you are (your authenticity).

So, here's a simple formula to make an assertive request:

Ask the person directly. Address them by name, and give the reason why you need help. Give a clear, short message about what you need from them. Make sure to stay calm, keep eye contact, and speak sincerely. Avoid being flattering to convince the person for help.

Be prepared to have a conversation until you both are satisfied. The other person also has the right to say "no" and ask for clarification, negotiate, or let you know about the problems your request might cause them. Be prepared for this.

Making requests assertively saves us from manipulating others or throwing our weight around and demanding assistance. It also builds our confidence and self-esteem. However, remember not to take the person's response to your requests personally.

Tips for being assertive

- EYE CONTACT – Look at the person to whom you talk most of the time, but don't stare at him 100 percent of the time.

- BODY POSTURE – Stand or sit up tall facing the person, but avoid being overly stiff.

- DISTANCE/PHYSICAL CONTACT – If you can feel the other person's breath, you are probably too close. Keep a comfortable distance from him.

- GESTURES – Use hand gestures to complement what you say, but remember you are not conducting an orchestra.

- FACIAL EXPRESSIONS – Ensure your facial expression matches your emotions and what you are saying. For example, don't laugh when you are upset or don't frown when you are happy.

- VOICE TONE, INFLECTION, and VOLUME – To make sure your assertive message is heard, pay attention to the tone of your voice, the inflection of your voice (emphasis on syllables), and its volume.

- FLUENCY – It's important to be fluent and let your words out efficiently.

- TIMING – Timing is important, especially when expressing your negative feelings or making a request to someone. Doing this several days later or immediately in front of people may not be the right time. Do it as soon as there is a time for both parties to resolve their issues alone.

- LISTENING is an important, yet often neglected part of assertiveness. When you express your feelings without infringing on the rights of others, you also need to give the other person a chance to respond.

- CONTENT – Depending upon what purpose you want to accomplish with your assertive behavior, the content of your message will be different.

How to handle criticism assertively

There are three ways to help you deal with the criticism and make a decision about which behavior, if any, you will change. Remember, people criticize your behavior - what you say and do, not who you are.

The three ways of handling criticism assertively are:

1. Agree, if it's true - It's always possible that there is some truth in what others say about you. For example, if someone says, "You always overthink petty issues," admit it, saying "Yes, sometimes I do tend to overthink on small matters."

2. If you made a mistake, accept it. Here, you are only saying about the mistake and nothing about yourself as a person. For example, your boss says "What's the matter with you, the file was supposed to be in .pdf" You admit your mistake and promise to correct it as soon as possible.

3. If somebody criticizes you unnecessarily, ask what exactly bothers him. For example, if someone criticizes your decision about late marriage. You agree that the marriage must happen at a certain age, but the person continues to make a big deal out of it. At this point, ask what it is exactly that concerns him.

Using any of the above three techniques for handling criticism assertively, you help yourself sail through an unpleasant situation without feeling guilty or dumb. Knowing that you can handle criticism without shouting or name-calling, it will allow you to become closer to the person you want to be.

Speak up for yourself and start thinking for yourself

Do you realize you are a unique, one-of-a-kind person? So you should learn how to feel comfortable in your skin, about the style in which you assert yourself. Some people speak loudly and enthusiastically, but people hear them clearly. But some speak more softly and infrequently, they are heard equally clearly.

So, don't change your style. The key is to put into words exactly what you want or need. So how can you make yourself heard?

- Look into the eyes of the person you talk to. If you are short or use a wheelchair, draw attention to yourself by speaking directly to the person. If the other person seems unwilling to look at you, find a clever, yet polite way to say, "I'm right here!"

- Speak clearly and distinctly. If you have a speech disability, calm your anxiety. Relax the body muscles, take in a deep breath and exhale slowly. Speak slowly and as distinctly as you can. You can visualize a soothing image such as a mountain stream to help you relax the body. When you are calm, the other person will also relax and concentrate on what you are saying.

- Be courteous and polite, but not obsequious.

- If the other person addresses everyone around except you, tell him nicely and firmly that you would like to be addressed directly.

- Think about what to say and how to say it, *before* you begin speaking.

Self-assessment: What's your style?

If being assertive is not your style, then what is? Pick any one option from below:

- The **Nice Guy,** who is afraid to say or do anything that might offend others.

- The **Whiner,** who constantly whines and complains about the things they need and are not receiving, how others treat them when they ask for anything, or how bad everything is, but never does anything about it.

- **Adherent Vine,** who expects others to stand up for your rights and intervene on your behalf.

- A **Silent Victim** who sulks silently and believes there's nothing they can change about their life.

- The **Fairy Princess** that expects everything to be delivered without any effort on their part.

- The **Waiter,** someone who is waiting for a miracle to happen. Who waits, waits, and waits for someone else to do something.

- The **Bombshell,** who sporadically fires angry missiles.

- The **Scared Cat,** who fears others will get onto them if they took the trouble to do something.

- The **Appeaser,** who settles with compromising his needs.

How do you view yourself when others criticize you?

What are your expectations when you ask someone for help?

Write answers to these questions before you learn more about assertiveness in the next chapter.

Chapter Summary

- Assertiveness is a mode of behavior and communication skill that can be learned and practiced to achieve what you want in life.

- The three keys to assertive behavior are: Know what you want, Say what you want, and Get what you want.

- Your body language speaks volumes about you and your confidence, even before you open your mouth. Make sure you exhibit confidence and assertiveness with your body language.

- Expressing your feelings, thoughts, and opinions, both positive and negative, saying "no" respectfully to certain requests, and asking for help when needed are the significant elements of assertive behavior.

In the next chapter you will learn:

- Why it's hard to say "no" to others

- How you can get better at saying "no" in life and business scenarios

- The right way to say "no"

CHAPTER FIVE

The Art of Refusing

One important aspect of assertive behavior is the ability to say "no" at the right time and in the right way. You know the benefits it has to you as a person and in your relationships. But, does knowing the benefits make everything easy?

You can't say "yes" to that! Right?

Why? Why is it hard to say no?

Jennie wasn't quite ready to get married. She knew her age was completely appropriate to tie the knot, but she wanted to focus on her career and think about marriage a year later. Her parents brought up the issue almost daily, "You are thirty-four now," they said. "If you delay, you won't find a good match. You'll have to spend your entire life alone. So why don't you think of getting married now?" Jennie knew her parents were probably right. However, somewhere inside, she wasn't completely convinced by the idea of marriage at the moment. And she didn't know how to say this to her parents.

Susan's friends were going to an expensive club. She couldn't afford to pay for a night out drinking, and also, didn't really want to get wasted, which she knew would be the end result of the evening. But she could not figure out how to get out of it without irritating all of her friends.

Susie had recently divorced her husband. Her parents and friends were pressuring her to sign up to a matrimonial site. But Susie was reluctant. Her problem was not if any guy will be interested in her or not, but what if she's not interested in them? She couldn't reject someone politely. She could not hurt other people's feelings. It was hard for her to say "no" to someone.

Do any of these situations seem familiar?

Many powerful men consider "no" to be an important part of a successful life strategy. For example,

Steve Jobs: *Focusing is about saying no.*

Warren Buffett: *We need to learn the slow yes and the quick no.*

Tony Blair: *The art of leadership is saying no, not saying yes. It is very easy to say yes.*

Despite these famous quotes by powerful men, it's not easy for us to develop the art of saying no. Why?

Here are the reasons:

Fear of conflict

Most of us are afraid of conflict. We don't like others to get angry with us or be critical of us. Therefore, we don't say "no" lest it might put us into conflict with someone else. Someone else may be our partner, a colleague, a friend, or the boss.

Many parents want to avoid battles with their children, and thus, fulfill all their demands, even if they know they shouldn't. They feel that if they said "no" to their children, their children will stop loving them.

However, this fear of conflict is taught to us as children. We are always taught and expected to do what parents, teachers, and others in power tell us. They show us the fear of punishment or losing their love if we don't obey. And this worry of conflict gets carried with us into adulthood.

Besides, the desire to fit in and be liked by our peers also prevents us from saying "no." Research shows that men and women have a tremendous need to belong to a peer group. We want to be accepted by our friends or the people we want to be friends with, and thus, stay mum.

Don't want to disappoint or hurt someone

Sometimes we do things that make others feel better, even if it's not what we want to do. But, just to make others smile, can you compromise your own? Imagine you have to submit an urgent project the next day but you can't say no to your relative for the party because you don't want to disappoint them.

Doesn't seem politically correct

For some, the idea of turning down someone's request is not politically correct as it presents you with being selfish and unconcerned.

Harder for women

Women often find it difficult to say "no" to men because they want to get along, want to be nice, and don't want to hurt their feelings.

It's a sign of weakness

Saying "no" is perceived by a few people as a sign of weakness, either in their own mind or in those for whom they work.

People don't expect you to say no

When someone asks you to do something, they already assume that you will say yes. So they already have a psychological advantage over you, and you don't wish to let down their expectations.

For example, let's say your mother asks you to cook dinner before you leave for the party at your friend's house. She knows you are running late, but she made the request because she wasn't feeling well that day. That seems okay! However, the problem arises when she asks you to cook dinner each time you have to attend to other important issues, even if she is feeling well.

How others will perceive you if you say no

You're afraid that if you say no, you'll be seen as someone who's difficult to get along with or someone who doesn't play well with others.

Well, your interests and the interests of those you work with might be radically different. But you give in to their interests and compromise with your own values so that people don't think poorly of you.

Saying yes is natural to you

Maybe you're just a "yes" type of person. That means it's consistent with your values. You don't agree with your boss just because he or she is your boss. Rather, it's embedded in your giving personality.

You like to be as helpful as possible whenever you can. You tend to think of others, their needs, and their time as being of greater value than your own. And so, it really doesn't matter what the request is. You'd simply rather say yes.

Though it seems to be a nice attitude, when taken to the extreme, it can grind you down. It's always good to take a balanced approach and preserve your time and energy as well. Only then you'll be able to help others in the way and to the extent you want to.

Saying yes is more positive than saying no

The world today is getting very negative. To have positivity in your life, you have to put it there, and so, you have to go out of your way to say no to the things you don't want to commit to.

Everyone else is saying yes

Now, what does that mean? Suppose you are at an office party and everyone is enjoying alcoholic drinks, except you. Because that's against your values. You don't drink alcohol at all. However, to avoid not fitting in with your colleagues, you trample your values. You can't dare to say no.

Inability to recognize the extent of the commitment

Suppose you keep taking on projects at your office. You didn't say no to any of them, thinking that you'll finish them all by the weekend. That happens because things seem super easy on the front end, but when you actually sit down to work on them, they're far more complicated.

To return a favor

Anytime someone does you a favor, you feel obligated to return it in some form. That's human psychology and the power of reciprocity. Now, there's nothing wrong with asking for or returning a favor. But you need to think over how you return it. You don't want to do something that's beyond your capacity or beyond the time you ought to spend on it.

To prove your worth

People with low self-esteem or insecurity in their jobs are usually more inclined to say yes to prove their worth.

Thus, you need to think before you accept any request, each and every time.

However, the point to remember is that these stated reasons are not facts. They are just the thoughts or opinions you have learned and grown up with. Each of these can be replaced by a powerful and true opinion about saying no.

What's the truth about saying "no"?

Replace your old thoughts and opinions about saying no with these:

- Others have the right to ask and I have the right to refuse. Don't be afraid that other people will get upset if you decline their request.

- Saying no is refusing the request, not rejecting the person.

- When I say "yes" to one thing, I actually say "no" to something else. I always have a choice.

- Problems arise because I overestimate the difficulty that the other person will have in accepting my refusal. But, if I express my feelings openly and honestly, the other person will also feel liberated to express his own.

- Saying "no" to someone's request doesn't mean he/she can't make further requests.

How you can get better at saying "no"

Once you have identified the personal reasons that stop you from saying "no," it's time to deploy these techniques:

- Practice saying "no" in small or unimportant situations, like not buying something at a drugstore.

- Stop for a minute and take a breath before saying "yes." This gives you a little space and time to assess and respond to your own needs.

- Seek other's advice if you need a backup for your own position. I'll talk more about this in a moment.

- Don't get trapped in the pitfall of "everyone else." It's almost universally true that everyone else is doing the same thing, or wants you to do whatever is being asked for.

- Take a minute and ask yourself if you'll feel guilt, anxiety, disappointment, or any other emotion if you don't do what's being asked for. Can you tolerate it? Is it worth it to accept the request in order not to feel those emotions?

- Assess the outcome. How bad will it be? Is it worth it to give in or not?

To get better at the art of saying no, remember that you can change your mind in most cases. Don't feel you only have one opportunity. There will be many more.

Getting a backup to say "no"

Most of us feel much better about saying "no" to someone if we have the backup of some buddies or the people we trust.

Continuing with the above examples,

Jennie talked to her friends about her parents' behavior towards marriage. They helped her to understand her parents' concerns but also taught her how to put into words how she feels about the issue.

Susie's friends offered her a variety of techniques for saying "no" to guys, like not answering their calls or giving some excuses to not move forward, but she didn't agree with them. She realized that saying "no" nicely but firmly is just a part of the process and doesn't make her a mean or bad person.

Susan also talked to a couple of friends who were not a part of the drinking group. They supported her decision that it's a waste of time, and you spend a ton of money on something that leaves you feeling miserable and affects your performance the next day. They told her that her friends won't even notice if she didn't go. They just want company.

Susan simply refused her friends, and after a couple of tries to change her mind, the girls left her alone. And there was no change in the way they treated her at work.

But, the toughest part comes now!

What's the right way to say no?

Even assertive people find themselves in situations where they say yes to things they really don't want to do. This can be appropriate in some situations. For example, if your boss asks you to do something, and you really don't want to do it, you can't practice your assertiveness skills and say no to him - you don't want to get fired!

But, suppose your friend asks you to do something that you just can't take out time for and you say yes, you'll find yourself over-loaded.

Now, let's take a look at some of the effects of not being able to say "no":

- You invite resentment and anger towards the person you have said "yes" to, though they have done nothing wrong. This resentment builds up over time to the point you can't tolerate it anymore.

91

- You become increasingly frustrated and disappointed with yourself.

- You can get overworked and highly stressed if you take more than you can cope with.

- In the long-term, you may have low self-esteem, depression, and anxiety.

- Under different circumstances, some people are able to say "no," but in an aggressive manner, without considering or respecting the other person. This may cause people to dislike and alienate you, which is not good assertive communication.

There are some basic principles to keep in mind when you want to say "no":

- Tell the person if you find it difficult to accept the request.

- Be straightforward and honest, but not rude.

- Be polite. Say something like "thank you for asking, but..."

- Keep your message brief. Don't over-explain your actions and reasons for saying no.

- Speak slowly with warmth and compassion.

- Don't apologize or give elaborate reasons for saying "no."

- Take responsibility for saying "no" and don't blame others or make excuses.

- If need be, provide alternatives to solve the other person's problem.

Remember, it's your right to say no if you don't want to do things. Plus, it's better to be truthful at the beginning than breed anger and resentment in yourself by saying "yes."

Suitable ways of saying "no"

There are a number of ways you can say "no" which are more appropriate according to the particular situations.

- **The direct "no"** - When someone asks you to do something you don't want to, just say 'no' without apologizing. Though forceful, this technique is quite effective with salespeople.

- **The reflecting "no"** - Here, you acknowledge the content and feel of the request, and then add your assertive refusal at the end. For example, "I know you're excited about the Goa trip, but I can't come."

- **The reasoned "no"** - In this technique, you give a brief and genuine reason for your refusal. For example, "I can't come shopping with you because I have to submit this assignment tomorrow."

- **The rain-check "no"** - It is not a definite "no." You may refuse the request at the present, but leave room for saying "yes" in the future. However, only use it if you genuinely want to meet the request. For example, "I can't come to meet your parents today, but I could make it sometime next week."

- **The enquiring "no"** - It's not a direct "no" but opening up the request to see if there is another way it could be met. For example, "Is there another dress I could buy for you?"

- **The broken record "no"** - Can be used in a wide range of situations where you repeat the simple statement of refusal over and over again. Without explanation, without apology, you keep repeating the refusal statement. It's particularly helpful with persistent requests.

How to say no in business scenarios

Ever notice how many times you accept a project and regret your decision later? Do all those projects actually align with your business goals?

If you can't refuse such projects, you'll pay the price. Missed deadlines, lost clients, physical and mental exhaustion, frustration, and stress. When you are habitual in accepting each and every request that comes your way, you lose focus and get unaligned from your goals. That's too high a price to pay.

So, learn how you can protect your time and energy in these typical business scenarios by knowing the right way to respond.

The freeloader is a pushy prospect who tries to persuade you and get his work done for free. Instruct him on the value of your work and how they can pay it.

Set up a formal consultation with the prospect, show your work plan, and determine whether you can work together. If things don't work

94

out your way, still, stay professional and friendly. You can share other resources in your network or recommend books, blogs, or courses. Your honesty and assistance will be appreciated by the prospect. Otherwise, there's nothing to lose as the prospect never intended to buy from you in the first place.

What do you call a client who always makes changes to the project? Even after signing on the proposal. A scope creeper! Such people often request changes that threaten to disturb the project's schedule and your sanity.

In such cases, be firm, clear, and upfront in the first meeting. Set clear boundaries for any ad hoc requests. Explain what your policies are on the post-signing of the project (such as rejection, time penalties, high cost, etc.). This ensures that the prospect will think twice before making any post-sign off requests.

The dead-end meeting. Incidental meetings clutter your calendar, are time-consuming, and leave you mentally exhausted. Before saying "yes" to any such meeting, assess how it will help in the progress of your project.

Take a minute to consult your schedule, analyze the pros and cons of the meeting, and then respond to the requestor with a confident answer. If it's not worth your time, simply say "no."

Or, if saying no is difficult or you want more information to make up your mind, seek it out before you commit. And finally, if you agree to a meeting, decide the time limit for the discussion.

How saying no helps you in a business setting

You gift yourself by saying "no" to the things you don't want to do. It reduces your calendar clutter and your anxiety, and you can focus -- both physically and mentally — on the things that really matter to your business. By saying "no" you protect your energy and the most important resource: TIME.

Saying "no" is a valuable asset.

Homework for you

Before you continue to the next unit, here's your homework:

1. Elaborate on one (or more) situation of your life where you want to say "no" but aren't able to.

2. Write one (or more) reason that stops you from saying "no."

3. Recall the conversation where you gave in to the request. What made you accept it? Then, imagine the same conversation and practice saying "no" with confidence.

Chapter Summary

- Saying "no" to others' requests at the right time and in the right way is crucial for your health, well-being, and for maintaining strong relationships.

- However, we fear saying "no" to others because we are afraid of conflicts, or that we might hurt or disappoint them by saying no.

- Anger, resentment, frustration, stress, depression, anxiety, and low self-esteem result from our inability to say "no" at the right time.

- Assertiveness teaches us how to respectfully say "no" to others while respecting our own needs.

In the next chapter you will learn:

- What boundaries are

- Why you should set boundaries for yourself

- Areas to set your boundaries

- How to set healthy boundaries?

CHAPTER SIX

How Are your Boundaries?

Unfortunately, the boundaries we set for ourselves aren't visible to others. They are not like a physical wall or a "no trespassing" sign we construct around ourselves. Nevertheless, you must set them, as well as let others know about them. That's essential for your health, mental wellbeing, and even safety.

You must set boundaries for:

- Personal space

- Sexuality

- Thoughts and feelings

- Possessions

- Time and energy

- Culture, religion, and ethics

Setting your boundaries and respecting those of others isn't rocket science, but still, you need to learn how to set them. Whether you want to set boundaries with your family or with strangers, here's how you can start.

Understanding and determining your boundaries

People usually misunderstand the word "boundary." They perceive them as a way to keep oneself separate from others. However, setting clear boundaries provides healthy rules for what you accept in relationships, personal or professional.

The benefits of setting your boundaries are:

Healthy relationships and enhanced self-esteem

Melissa Coats, a licensed professional counselor says that *"Boundaries protect relationships from becoming unsafe. They actually bring us closer together than take farther apart, and are therefore necessary in every relationship."*

Having boundaries allows you to prioritize yourself, whether in self-care, career, or relationships.

Boundaries should be flexible

Boundaries shouldn't be drawn in permanent ink. You must reassess them from time to time and make the necessary changes. Too rigid, or too inflexible of boundaries give rise to problems rather than benefits.

Boundaries help to conserve your emotional energy

When you can't advocate for yourself, you seem to lose your identity. Your self-esteem dwindles. You build bitterness toward others. However, when you set your boundaries, you are at peace and conserve your energy for self-care.

Boundaries provide you a space to grow

Our feelings are not always that simple. It sometimes feels complicated. Setting the boundaries and breaking them when required shows your vulnerability. Simply talking about your complex feelings openly with your friends displays your authenticity. And when you do so, you welcome others to open up to you when they need to.

However, vulnerability and oversharing are different. Vulnerability is genuine and brings people closer. On the contrary, oversharing blackmails emotionally and forces the relationship over another person.

Pointers to oversharing are:

- Attacking someone personally on social media

- Not using a filter to who views your daily dramas on social media

- Sharing personal details with new people in the hope of hurrying the friendship along

- Dominated, one-sided conversations

- Expecting friends and family to give you on-call emotional therapy

By oversharing, you could be trampling other people's boundaries.

How to set your boundaries

Setting your boundaries is not a tutorial you can search on Google. Each one of us has their own set of boundaries that vary from one person to another.

What shapes our boundaries?

- Our heritage or culture

- Where we live in or come from

- Whether we are introverts, extroverts, or somewhere in between

- Our life experiences

- Our family dynamics

We all have a different family dynamic. Each of us understands situations differently. And we all change our boundaries as we grow older and shift our perspective. One size doesn't fit all.

Self-reflection helps in setting your own boundaries. It includes the knowledge of:

1. What are your rights?

Identify your basic human rights when setting your boundaries. These include:

- Right to say no without feeling guilty.

- Right to be treated with respect.

- Right to give equal importance to your and other's needs.

- Right to accept your mistakes and failures.

- Right to deny others' unreasonable expectations.

Once you are aware of your rights and believe in them, it gets easier to honor them. When you honor them, you'll stop spending energy pleasing others who don't respect your rights.

102

2. What do your instincts tell you?

You can clearly make out when someone violates your boundaries or when you need to set one based on your gut feelings. Signs like an increased heart rate, sweating, chest tightness, and stomach uneasiness tell you that you aren't comfortable in a situation and must draw a boundary. For example, do you clench your fists when you find your roommate reading your journal? Does someone asking about your married life make you tighten your jaw?

3. What values do you have?

Your boundaries and your morals are closely related. Identify your ten important values and pick out the three most significant ones. What challenges do these values face that make you feel uncomfortable? This tells you if you have set strong and healthy boundaries for yourself.

Setting your boundaries – taking action

Tips to confidently establish your boundaries:

1. Use assertiveness

Assertively setting boundaries exhibits your firm stance and, is actually being kind to others. With assertive language, you are not harsh, but non-negotiable, without criticizing the recipient. Aggressive language, on the other hand, seems harsh and pushy.

Using "I statements" reflect assertiveness. It shows confidence and sets a good boundary by expressing your thoughts and feelings without fear.

For example, consider these two sentences:

First: *Keep your hands off my diary!*

Second: *I feel encroached upon when you see my diary because it's my private space where I pen down my thoughts.*

Which one do you think allows others to respect your privacy? The second one, of course. Because it's clear, non-negotiable, and expresses what you want and why.

2. Develop the habit of saying no

As discussed earlier, by saying "no," you bless yourself. You don't need to explain yourself to the person you are refusing.

3. Protect your spaces

Set boundaries for your personal stuff, physical and emotional spaces, as well as your time and energy. Take the help of your tech gadgets for this.

- Lock your private items in a drawer or box.

- Instead of a paper journal, use a password-protected digital journal.

- Schedule non-negotiable alone time or time when you do things you love.

- Use passwords or other security features on devices and tech accounts.

- Set aside a specific time for answering emails or texts.

- Use the "out of office" responder on email accounts when on a vacation.

- Send verification of your time off days in advance.

- Temporarily delete email and messaging apps when you don't want to be contacted.

- Use the "Do Not Disturb" feature on your phone and other devices.

- Promise yourself not to respond to messages or calls sent to personal accounts.

Others may expect us to reply to work emails during non-work hours. However, this can take a toll on your wellbeing and relationships. So, strive to create a balance between your work and personal life each time you can.

As an adult, you also have the right to secure the privacy of your mail accounts and messages. Communicate your boundaries to others about your digital devices as well.

4. Ask for assistance

If you are mentally ill, depressed, anxious, or have experienced any trauma, it may be hard for you to define and assert your boundaries. In such cases, reach out for help from a mental health professional.

How to recognize and honor other people's boundaries

As important as it is to honor our own boundaries, it is equally important to recognize and honor others, lest we might overstep them.

But, how do we do this? Just follow these three rules:

1. Check the clues

Taking note of social cues helps you identify others' boundaries. If someone is uncomfortable with closeness, they'll step back when you step forward while talking to them.

These are some clues that others want more space:

- No eye contact

- Turning away or sideways

- Taking a step back

- Short response to conversation

- Excessive nodding

- Sudden high-pitched voice

- Gestures that reflect nervousness like talking with hands or talking fast

- Folding arms or stiffening the posture

- Cringing

2. Watch out for neurodiverse behaviors

Neurodiversity or neurodiverse behaviors are shown by people with autism, dyslexia, ADHD, and other developmental disabilities. Such people use certain gestures all the time or have poor eye contact or difficulty starting a conversation. Look out for such behaviors when talking with someone who has developmental disabilities.

3. Seek permission

Never underestimate the power of questioning. Always enquire before engaging in physical touch, like a hug, or if you can ask a personal question to the person.

Boundaries are there to help us

Setting boundaries should be thought of as bracing our relationships with others rather than building walls to keep people out. And boundaries help us much beyond that. They can give us a clue about damaging behaviors. We often neglect our instincts thinking them to be unreasonable, but if something constantly feels uncomfortable or unsafe, it's a sign of trouble.

If anyone pushes or violates your boundaries, again and again, pay attention. Also ask people in your life to honestly tell you if you push their boundaries accidentally.

Sometimes boundaries don't work

Setting boundaries is an advanced form of assertiveness. It involves taking a position about who you are, what you're willing to do or not do, and how you want to be treated in your relationships.

However, even if you have set your limits, sometimes they don't work! Despite your efforts, your boundaries are often ignored or crossed! It frustrates you, but it's not always the other person's fault. Here's why your boundaries don't work despite communicating them assertively:

- You set the boundary in anger or by nagging, for example, "I've told you a hundred times..."

- Your tone is blaming or critical rather than firm.

- You didn't set consequences for violating your boundary.

- You withdraw assertion when challenged with reason, anger, threats, name-calling, or silent treatment.

- Your consequences are too frightening or unrealistic to carry out.

- You don't appreciate the importance of your needs and values sufficiently.

- You don't exercise consequences on a consistent basis, i.e., each time your boundary is violated.

- You give in to sympathize with the other person's pain and place his or her feelings and needs above your own.

- Your consequences insist others must change. Consequences aren't meant to punish someone or change their behavior, but rather require you to *change your behavior*.

- You lack a support system to reinforce *your new behavior.*

- Your words and actions contradict each other. Remember, actions speak louder than words. Actions that reward someone for violating your boundary prove that you aren't serious. For example:

❖ You tell your neighbor to always call first before coming to your apartment, and then you allow her to come into your house uninvited.

❖ Telling someone not to call after nine in the evening, but answer the phone.

❖ Telling your colleagues not to send emails on Sunday, but answering them on Sunday.

❖ Nagging or complaining about unwanted behavior, but not taking any action.

What you can do?

While setting boundaries, it's critical that you identify your feelings, needs, and values (e.g., honesty, fidelity, privacy, and mutual respect). Do you honor or override them? Once you know your comfort zone, you can determine your boundaries easily. Assess your current boundaries in all areas by thinking about:

• What specific behaviors have you allowed that violate your values or compromise your needs and wants?

• How does it affect you and your relationships?

• Can you put in the risk and effort to maintain your boundaries?

• What are the rights you believe you have?

• Have you said or done something that didn't work? Why?

- What are the consequences you can live with if someone violates your boundaries? Always keep your word and follow through with consequences. Don't give empty threats.

- How will you handle the other person's reaction?

To maintain your limits and make them work, you need to have the conviction that the limit is necessary and appropriate. This conviction comes by realizing how much you have to pay in relationships and health by not having the limits in place.

Areas you need to set boundaries

There are several areas where boundaries apply:

- Material boundaries to determine giving things such as your money, cars, clothes, books, food, etc.

- Physical boundaries to safeguard your personal space, privacy, and body. Do you give a handshake or a hug – to whom and when? How do you react to loud music, nudity, or locked doors?

- Mental boundaries apply to your thoughts, values, and opinions. Do you know what you believe? Can you hold on to your opinions? Can you open-mindedly listen to someone else without becoming rigid?

- Emotional boundaries distinguish separating your emotions and their responsibility from others. Healthy boundaries prevent you from blaming others or accepting blame. You don't shoulder your negative feelings over someone else. They also protect you from feeling guilty for others' negative feelings and taking their comments personally. If you react with strong emotions, arguments, or defensive mode, you may have weak emotional boundaries.

- Sexual boundaries protect your comfort level with sexual touch and activity.

- Spiritual boundaries relate to your beliefs and experiences in connection with a supreme power.

Internal boundaries

Internal boundaries regulate your relationship with yourself. Consider them self-discipline and healthy management of time, thoughts, emotions, behavior, and impulses.

If you procrastinate or do things you neither have to nor want to do, or overwork without getting enough rest, you are neglecting your internal physical boundaries. If you can't manage your negative thoughts and feelings and stay in balance, you have weak internal emotional boundaries.

Healthy physical and emotional internal boundaries help you to not obsess about other people's feelings and problems. You think and prioritize yourself, rather than agreeing with others' criticism or advice. Since you're accountable for your feelings and actions, you don't blame others. If you're blamed and you don't feel responsible, instead of defending yourself or apologizing, you can say, "I don't take responsibility for that."

Guilt and resentment

If you feel resentful or victimized and blame people or situations in your life, it means you haven't set your boundaries. If you feel anxious or guilty about setting them, remember your relationships may suffer when you do. Setting boundaries makes you feel empowered, less anxious, and without resentment or guilt. In addition, you receive more respect from others and your relationships improve.

How to set healthy boundaries

Take the following steps:

Remember, no boundaries = little self-esteem

Self-awareness and being assertive are the first steps to set your boundaries. Your boundaries are your values. Boundaries show others how much or how little you respect yourself. Boundaries are your best friend.

Decide what your core values are.

Who are you? What are your values? What's your comfort zone and what exactly makes you feel uncomfortable? For example, I don't like to be disturbed when I'm working on my laptop. So, I set my phone to "do not disturb" while I'm working. In my relationships, I value and expect honesty, quality time, and one hundred percent transparency. Once you are clear on what matters most to you, you can take the next step of communicating this to others.

Pro tip: Instead of creating your boundaries around a difficult relationship, make your boundaries about you. For example, my boundary with my phone time is about honoring the fact that I tend to lose focus if I am distracted during my busy writing schedule. This boundary is to decrease my stress and frustration, and not about avoiding phone calls.

You can't change others, but you can change yourself

We all want others to change. We get into arguments with our partners, parents, or peers, hoping and expecting them to change. Though we know we can't change others, we still sometimes try. So always remind yourself that you are not responsible for what comes out of someone else's mouth, the choices they make, or their reactions.

Bottom line?

Since you can't change other people, change the way you deal with them. When we change our ways, the world around us will change, too.

Brahma Kumaris, a spiritual organization, always recommends to first change *your* thoughts about the other person and to think positively about them no matter how they behave. This changes your behavior towards them, and they are motivated to change themselves. Doesn't this chain reaction sound good?

Decide the consequences ahead of time

So what do you do if someone pushes your boundaries (because they will)? Decide the consequences beforehand and communicate it clearly. However, don't make empty threats or give in if others violate your boundaries.

For example, if my friend calls me repeatedly during my work time, I simply do not answer the phone. The best way to figure out your own boundaries and consequences of violating them is to sit quietly with yourself and make this all about you. Remember, boundaries are about honoring *your* needs, not about judging other people's choices.

Let your behavior speak for you

Present your boundaries clearly to people and then let your behavior do the talking. People *will* test, push, and disrespect your limits. But you need to stick to it and follow through with the consequences you've set forth each and every time someone violates the boundaries you've set for yourself.

When you don't react in anger for violating your boundaries, it indicates a healthier you, emotionally and physically.

Say what you mean, and mean what you say

You may have set the healthiest of boundaries for yourself, but if you do not communicate them clearly, you are going to make them easy to manipulate. Moreover, it will create confusing relationships, for you and everyone involved.

When you say one thing and do another, people get an opportunity to question your character or authenticity. Why take such a chance?

Sometimes, we're afraid to confront our loved ones and tell them the truth about our feelings. We're scared to admit that we hate going to certain restaurants, or have trouble spending time with a friend's toxic cousin, or hate when a boss dumps deadline on us at six o'clock on a Friday.

But, keep in mind: the more you ground yourself with your boundaries and values, the more clearly you'll be able to communicate them to others.

How to talk about your boundaries: ASSA Technique

Ding dong!

Yes, that's your doorbell! But what if it rings at an unreasonable hour? What if it's also from the same person every time?

My mother, a passionate housewife, really gets disturbed by this. Do you know why? Blame it on our neighbor. Every other day, at 2:30 p.m., her kids ring the doorbell to enquire about where their mother is, or if she has left the house key with us. And that's my mom's nap time. She gets up early in the morning at 4:30 a.m. and finishes all her chores. Post-lunch she feels the need to relax and take a little nap.

Thanks to the neighbor and her kids, she can't make it to an undisturbed nap most of the time. She has informed her neighbor several times about her nap but to no avail.

"Can't she give the extra key of the house to her kids? They are mature enough. Or why is she not at home by the time her kids come from the school? They disturb my sleep every day." That's what my Mom mutters to herself frequently. Of course, she would because she has reacted passively to such behavior from our neighbor. She doesn't want to yell at them, but telling them not to disturb hasn't worked either.

So, should she continue to accept their behavior? Or should she shout and make them follow through?

Well, none of these options seem to be the right choice! Being passive and accepting the boundary-crossing behavior makes her furious; it's only that she doesn't express it. But she won't be able to hold it in for long. And yelling won't help. It will only spoil the relationship.

Does this sound familiar to you? Or do you face a similar situation? How do you tackle it? How should you handle people when they take you for granted?

Follow these 5 steps:

Step 1: Define your boundaries

Decide your limits and stick to them. What behaviors are you willing to accept from other people and what are you not? This doesn't mean rigidity, but have a limit and stick to it.

Step 2: Forgiveness doesn't mean not taking action

Most of us have a forgiving nature. That's what has been taught to us. Forgiveness is a quality of courageousness and helps people change. But, if you continually forgive someone for their bad behavior, they get much worse. This, of course, doesn't do them any good. Constantly forgiving and allowing bad behavior ceases to *be* a "bad behavior" in the eyes of the person doing it.

Research shows that people who insult their spouses, throw items, or exhibit any type of violence get more aggressive if their partners repeatedly forgive them for it.

Though forgiveness can compel others to change, it has to be accompanied by appropriate action. By appropriate, I don't mean acting aggressively, but setting a limit on your tolerance.

So how do you set this limit to their bad behavior?

Step 3: Practice the ASSA technique

Practicing assertiveness needs a strategy, whether it's with your colleague, a disrespectful partner, or a cranky neighbor. Assertiveness is a calm, clear communication, and not a verbal onslaught.

Often when we are upset with someone's behavior, we shout or scream, but they genuinely might not know the reason for our bad mood. Don't expect people to read your mind and just *know* that you are upset. Tell them about your bad mood, and the reason for it.

Follow the "ASSA" technique, which stands for:

Alert the person that you wish to speak to them. For example: "I want to talk to you about the backtalk you do in front of my friends." You don't blame or use any emotional language to make your point.

State your problem. What and why it's a problem: "I don't like it when you shout back at me. It makes me feel insulted and I think it makes you look rude in front of my friends."

Sell the benefits of better behavior. Say "In the future, if you disagree with me, it'd be better for you to have a private conversation with me. This will make you appear more mature and resolve our conflict."

Agree to behave differently in the future. "Shall we agree that from now on, you won't backtalk me? If you wish to have a word with me, you'll do it privately in our room?"

In the future, if ever they repeat the bad behavior, remind them what you had agreed upon.

Notice the clarity of this type of communication. You've neither passively accepted their bad behavior nor lost your cool and insulted them.

This type of assertive communication is a powerful method to correct someone's bad behavior. Though they might not change their ways (not immediately at least), you have given them an opportunity to behave better and openly communicated your boundaries.

Step 4: Stay calm

That's super important. When people overstep your limits, it's natural to lose your cool. But you can handle the situation with a little presence of mind. And for that, you need to be *calm*. The moment you start criticizing or yelling or sobbing, you invite defensiveness from the opposite side. Staying calm in such a situation takes practice. That's why it's important you rehearse what you're going to say.

Step 5: Practice honesty

We've all received an appalling gift from a relative or friend, and even if we didn't like it, we pretend that it's awesome. Because we think that being honest may hurt their feelings. But, by being honest, you'll gain more respect for yourself and others. Ultimately, it will help the other person to seriously look at their behavior and assess it. People won't be forced to live under the illusion that their behavior is okay when it really isn't.

Sometimes you need to use a clear, concise, and direct language.

How about you?

1. Have you set your boundaries at work and in relationships? If not, what stops you from doing it?

2. What are the situations where you feel people overstep your boundaries?

3. How do you react to people who do so? Do you forgive them and let them cross your boundaries again, or take concrete action?

Chapter Summary

- You can set boundaries for your personal space, possessions, sexuality, thoughts and feelings, time and energy, culture, religion, and ethics.

- Setting your healthy boundaries and respecting those of others improve your self-esteem, conserve your emotional energy, gives you a space to grow, and build healthy relationships.

- However, your boundaries won't work if you set them in anger, make them too rigid, get critical about others, or don't set a consequence for overriding them.

- Convey and assert your boundaries using the ASSA technique.

In the next chapter you will learn:

- Why it's difficult to express your feelings

- Tips for opening up about your feelings

- Techniques for expressing yourself

- Assertive communication formula

CHAPTER SEVEN

Assertive Self-expression

Expressing what and how you feel is the second category of assertive behavior. However, openly expressing feelings easily doesn't come naturally to everyone. Men typically have a more difficult time expressing their emotions, but almost everyone at one time or another in their life finds it difficult to say how they feel.

When it's difficult to express how you feel

When you learn why you have trouble expressing your feelings, it goes a long way into changing that behavior. You can learn how to express your feelings, just as readily as you can learn how to fix a faucet or mend a button on a shirt.

Here are the nine common reasons people find it difficult to express their emotions to others:

You don't know exactly what you feel

A person might be experiencing feelings such as sadness, rejection, disrespect, hurt, or shame, but it's better to be precise. Knowing exactly what you feel helps you connect with yourself, the values you have, and those you wish to live by. It also increases the likelihood of being understood by others.

Fear of conflict

We are afraid of angry feelings or conflicts with people. You believe that people with good relationships should not engage in verbal "fights" or intense arguments. Plus, you fear disclosing your thoughts and feelings to those you care about would result in their rejection of you.

This is sometimes referred to as the "ostrich phenomenon" — burying your head in the sand instead of addressing relationship problems.

Emotional perfectionism

Some people believe that they should not have feelings such as anger, jealousy, depression, or anxiety. They think they should always be rational and in control of their emotions. Expressing these emotions will present them as weak and vulnerable. You fear that people will criticize or reject you if they know how you really feel.

Fear of disapproval and rejection

People are so terrified by rejection and ending up alone that they would rather swallow their feelings, and put up with some abuse rather than expressing them. They feel an excessive need to please others and to meet their expectations. Such people are afraid that others won't like if they expressed their thoughts and feelings.

Passive-aggressive behavior

Passive-aggressive behavior makes you pout and hold your hurt or angry feelings inside instead of disclosing them. You give others the silent treatment, which is inappropriate, and a common strategy to elicit the feelings of guilt on their part.

Hopelessness

When you are convinced that your relationship cannot improve no matter what you do, you stop expressing yourself. You feel that you have already tried everything, and nothing works. You blame your spouse (or partner) for being too stubborn and insensitive to be able to change.

These beliefs represent a self-fulfilling prophecy–once you give up, an established position of hopelessness supports your predicted outcome.

Low Self-Esteem

Due to low self-esteem, people feel they are not entitled to express their feelings or to ask others for what they want. You always try to please other people and meet their expectations in such a case.

Spontaneity

Only when you are upset, you have the right to say what you think and feel. If that's what you believe, you express feelings only at that time, and none other. However, during a calm and structured or semi-structured exchange, if you express your feelings, it does not result in a perception that you are "faking" or attempting to inappropriately manipulate others.

Mind Reading

You expect others to know how you feel and what you need (although you have not disclosed it to them yet). This expectation provides an excuse to engage in non-disclosure, and thereafter, feel resentful because people do not appear to care about your needs.

Martyrdom

You are afraid to admit that you are angry, hurt, or resentful because you don't want to give anyone the satisfaction of knowing that their behavior affects you. You take pride in controlling your emotions and experiencing hurt or resentment, which obviously does not support clear and functional communication.

Tips for Opening Up

Once you've explored why you have such a hard time expressing yourself, you can work on doing so more effectively and confidently. Here are a few tips which will help you feel more comfortable about opening up about your feelings:

1) Be clear about your desire to share your feelings

Ask yourself why you want to share your feelings in the first place. Do you expect the other person to change? Do you share to vent? Or do you want advice? Or are you sharing for self-exploration?

Be clear regarding your reasons and expectations whether sharing feelings with a therapist, friend, or a loved one.

2) Acknowledge the intimacy of sharing feelings

Before going into the actual conversation about your feelings, it's important you acknowledge that sharing is intimate. Your history of trust in others and yourself influences your openness to share your feelings.

3) Start small

If you don't feel comfortable discussing your feelings, don't dive in headfirst. Instead, first experiment by sharing those things that are least uncomfortable to share.

4) Begin with the people you trust most

Begin expressing your feelings with the people you trust most: a best friend, a sibling, or a parent.

5) Be mindful of the experience

Notice the experience you get by sharing your feelings so that you can make the next one even better. What part felt comfortable? Does it make you more likely to share the next time? If not, what do you need to feel more comfortable in sharing your feelings?

6) Remember the harmful effects of suppressed feelings

Lastly, remember that keeping your feelings bottled up inside doesn't do any good. Suppressing, minimizing, or denying your feelings make you less available to recognize them in others. In contrast, acknowledging your feelings increases your empathy. Recognizing and acknowledging your pain is a form of empathy. This awareness heightens your capacity for empathy with others.

Techniques for expressing yourself

Often people associate expressive assertiveness with standing up for your rights when you feel that someone has taken advantage of you in a negative way. However, being more assertive can also help you to move ahead in a positive way, toward your goals.

Assertiveness can help you:

- Speak up in meetings when you want to

- Say "no" when you don't want to do something, or

- Express positive goals and request the required resources to make them happen

Will you get what you want by communicating assertively? Well, there's no guarantee, but you will have the satisfaction of expressing yourself in a positive, self-advocating way. You'll feel better about yourself and your communication with others. This will increase the probability of getting what you need or want if you can express exactly what it is.

Techniques for assertive expression:

Plan in advance what you are going to say. Visualize the scene and be positive.

Use "I statements" to express yourself. "I statements" help you focus on your own thoughts, feelings, and needs as well as acknowledge those of others. The real focus in I statements is on the "I feel," "I want," or "I think" part of the statement. Identifying your thoughts, feelings, and wants related to a situation keeps you from blaming someone else or getting caught up in the emotion of the moment. Avoid words that weaken the power of your messages like *could, sorry, not usually, maybe, suppose, possible, perhaps, er...* or *um...*

For example, "When you shout at me, I feel upset and put down, which negatively affects how I work. I would like you to speak to me properly, and with a normal tone so that I can do my job better."

Stick to it like a broken record.

Repeat your request several times so that your message is considered to be important. Don't give up if it was rejected at first.

For example, after you have requested your file to be reviewed and have not had a response, "I understand that you are very busy with... I value your input on my project file so that I can move ahead to finish my assignment."

Be empathetic and acknowledge others' feelings

For example, "I know you want the assignment to be delivered tomorrow, but I seriously can't, as I have other important issues to attend to."

State the consequence of not changing behavior

For example, "If you do not allow sufficient time to write the content, it will be less effective than you need it to be, and I'll have to write it again. I'd prefer not to do that."

Respond to criticism in a non-defensive way.

When someone criticizes you, they expect you to disagree or resist what they say, and to respond in a defensive way. However, you can put critical comments in perspective and still respect your point of view. You can agree with some part of what was said without being defensive.

For example: If someone says "That was a poor presentation you gave at the meeting." You might respond by saying, "Yes, I can see that I have some areas that could be improved."

If you can agree with some areas of criticism, you can respond by seeking to understand what is leading to criticism. Continuing with the above example, you could ask about what could be improved and say, "Actually, I could have been better. What do you think could be improved?"

Acknowledge your weaknesses or mistakes

That's called "negative assertion." We all have areas where we can improve. However, we can acknowledge our mistakes and weaknesses without being self-demeaning.

Assertive communication formula: Sending the message clearly

Confidence and assertiveness are often thought to mean the same thing. However, they are different in many ways.

Assertiveness is conducting yourself with confidence and not hesitating to express your desires and beliefs. Confidence is defined as the trait of being certain of yourself and your abilities.

The main difference between the two is communication. You can be assertive only if there is someone or something for you to be assertive towards, whereas confidence can exist inwardly and in isolation.

Assertiveness cannot exist without underlying confidence and can only exist in a situation where there is communication. Assertiveness can be portrayed through strong body language, tone of voice, and expressions. Confidence, on the other hand, needs nothing to aid in its existence. Put simply, you can be confident without being assertive, but you can't be assertive without being confident.

Thus, speaking up and expressing yourself can be difficult, sometimes overwhelming if you are shy, lack confidence, or come from a culture where it is inappropriate to speak up. It can also feel awkward and unnatural if you're more inclined to voice your frustrations and discontent in an indirect or passive manner.

But, remember, while fears about speaking up are hard, they are not impossible to overcome. Using an "assertiveness formula" can help.

This assertiveness formula can be applied to any situation at your home or in the workplace. Let's learn the three parts of the assertive communication formula.

Start with a short, simple, objective statement about the other person's behavior. For example: "When you interrupt me during my work..." Here your goal is to get the other person's attention without triggering their defensiveness. The statement should be short, to the point, and unemotional enough to let them hear your message and not immediately disagree or disengage.

Describe the negative effects of their behavior. Explain why the person's behavior is causing you a problem. For example, if the first part of the formula is "When you interrupt me during my work," you can add, "I lose the flow of my ideas." The goal here is to build a cause-and-effect logic. Link an objective statement of their behavior to the impact that behavior has on you.

End with a feelings statement. Here, you must indicate how their offending behavior has not only negatively impacted your actions but also hurt your feelings. An example of a feelings statement might be "I feel anxious" or "I feel distracted."

Putting it all together, you'll have something like this: "When you continually interrupt me during my work, I lose the flow of my ideas, and I feel anxious."

Of course, even with a formula in hand, assertiveness isn't always easy. It's quite possible that the recipient of your message may react negatively, so you must meet any response with a calm, steady, and confident presence.

What you can do is to accumulate as much evidence as possible to support your statement about the other person's offending behavior. You might keep track of instances when you felt hurt, undermined, or offended by the person's actions. Don't use this record to nag at the other person. Only use it as backup material if your counterpart refutes you and needs convincing. This evidence will increase the likelihood that your message will be heard and ultimately have the intended effect on the recipient.

One thing to remember is that there's no one-size-fits-all version of the message. You can, and should, tweak it to your own style to make the message feel as authentic as possible.

Speaking up is genuinely hard for many of us. And the results are far from guaranteed. The other person may respond in a positive way immediately; or respond positively and productively but with a significant delay; or might not respond at all. But for you, getting the courage to voice your opinions and frustrations in the first place is a significant win.

Homework for you

Answer the following questions before proceeding to the next chapter.

1. What stops you from speaking up about your feelings to others?

2. If ever you expressed your feelings, what was the response from the other person?

3. How likely are you to express your feelings to the same person (or others) in the future?

Chapter Summary

- People find it difficult to express their emotions because they can't figure out exactly what they feel. Plus, the fear of conflict, disapproval, and rejection, or emotional perfectionism, passive-aggressive behavior, or low self-esteem also stop them from expressing themselves.

- Once you are clear on your feelings to share, begin by sharing things that are least uncomfortable to share. Share with people you trust the most: a best friend, a sibling, or a parent.

- To express yourself assertively, first plan what you are going to say. Start with a small, objective statement about the undesirable behavior, describe how it affects you, and ultimately, how you feel. Remember to stay calm and empathetic throughout the discussion.

In the next chapter you will learn:

- How to ask for what you want

- ERPG/Assertive request formula

- How to ask for a raise

- Tips for assertive questioning

CHAPTER EIGHT

Ask and Receive What You Want

Asking for what you want

Many of us find it incredibly difficult to ask for things, especially at work, even though the request is completely fair. You may wonder what your colleagues will think of you. Will you sound greedy? Presumptuous? Will it irritate them? The list is endless!

If you have a lot of trouble asking for things, here are seven tips on how to ask for what you want:

Let go of the guilt

Let go of your guilt when making a request. Guilt usually surrounds those that are people-pleasers and dislike causing inconvenience to anyone. Always remind yourself that asking for things is not greedy. It's not wrong, rather it is healthy self-care.

Start small

Start small, like asking for a different table at a restaurant. This way you'll get used to how it feels to make a small, simple request. You'll also begin to realize that nothing bad will happen when you voice your needs.

Don't assume others to be mind-readers

We often assume our spouse, boss, work colleagues, or even our friends can read our minds. So when they don't act our way, we end up being hurt and upset. For any relationship to thrive, both parties have to take responsibility for clearly communicating their needs.

Be aware of the person you're asking

Psychologist Susan Krauss Whitbourne wrote that we must, "be conscious of the person we are asking and their needs, as opposed to solely focusing on what you want out of a situation." Put yourself in the other person's shoes, and you'll be able to frame your request in a way that is also beneficial to the other person, thus, increasing the likelihood of getting a positive answer.

However, if you put off the request because the timing never seems right, perhaps it's your own feelings of inadequacy or insecurity that prevent you from stepping forward.

Be honest

Honesty is always the best policy. Honestly express what you need and why you need it, and assure the other person that there won't be any rule changes down the road.

Ask and you shall receive... but you have to ask

It's said that "if you want something, you have to ask for it and risk not getting it, otherwise the chance of not getting it is definitely one hundred percent." Just imagine the things you might not have in life if you don't stick your neck out; from jobs, to pay raises, to simply getting someone's autograph.

Imagine the worst possible outcome

When you're afraid to ask for something, take a deep breath and imagine the worst possible outcome. Usually, it will be a simple "no" from the other side, which is not exactly life-threatening. I used this tactic when asking for my pay raise and it definitely helped. At worst, my recruiters would politely tell me, no, but I'd still have a job that I was pretty happy to go to every day. Struggling with the simple task of vocalizing what you want can be incredibly frustrating, but the good news is it's a skill you can improve and finesse over time.

Assertive request formula

If you wish to make an assertive request to someone to change their behavior or get what you want, there's a simple "ERPG" formula to use. ERPG stands for Empathy, Respect, Problem, and Goal.

Before you apply the formula, it's ideal to have a clear understanding of our goals. Be clear in your mind as to how you want others to behave, what action to take, what their reaction could be, and how you'll respond. If possible, place an assertive request at the place and time convenient to you.

ERPG formula

Establish Empathy and Respect and state positive feelings

Before making the request, try to understand the other person's feelings, and communicate that you do.

For example, "I know you won't be able to hire another freelance writer for this assignment at a short notice, but I hope you'll understand that I am currently overworked."

Show your respect and care for the person, and acknowledge the parts of their behavior that are likely to keep your conversations positive and out of blaming territory.

For example, "I appreciate your support to ensure timely payments for all my assignments."

State the problem and negative feelings

Speak in a manner that convinces them to solve your problem and not turn against you. Ask for their help, but don't blame your negative feelings on them. If you're upset with their behavior, remember that it's your own feelings, your own way of reacting to their behavior that you can control. However, that said, you can still express your problem, negative feelings, and ask for their help.

For example, "When you continually blame me for my past mistakes, it hurts me and I start defending myself instead of addressing the real issue."

State the goal and request new behavior

Sometimes just expressing the problem is not enough. You may have to speak about the problem, as well as the goal you wish to achieve.

State the kind of new behavior you want and how it would affect you. But, let others choose their new behavior as much as possible. When things are in their hands, they are more likely to help and suggest solutions to the problem. The other person may even think of a better solution than you. This approach gets them to be considerate of your problem and help solve it rather than turning defensive.

For example, "Instead of blaming me for my past mistakes, you could describe what I did and how I can improve in the future. Then, I would feel less defensive and more accommodating of your suggestions."

Follow-up after making the request

If the person avoids your request, attacks you, gets manipulative, makes you feel guilty or angry, makes excuses, or simply refuses to do it, use other assertive techniques such as the broken record, disarming anger, or making a contract.

While making a contract, clearly jot down the points of agreement (and possibly the points of disagreement). The agreement should be written and signed by both parties.

While following the above steps of ERPG formula, make sure you use an assertive style of communication. Don't put yourself or others in a defensive mode. Try to stay calm, rational, and helpful as much as possible.

- Use words like "keep doing what you're doing" or "didn't do it the way I wanted it to be" or "you waited for me to make the decision" or "give me negative feedback."

- Avoid using critical words like poor job, dependent, unworthy, or profanity

- Pay attention to non-verbal responses like good eye contact

- Use "I statements"

- Be direct

- Reduce hesitation words

- Stick to the issues

- Maintain an understanding, caring, yet firm stance

The above steps of the formula can be summarized into a sentence like:

I understand/like.............; however, when you................, I feel.......... I would appreciate it if you would.................

Asking for a raise

Besides asking for new behavior, asking for a pay raise is yet another struggle. You know that you've added a lot of value to your company or organization, and you feel entitled to a raise.

So, how do you request a raise confidently and in a manner that is likely to succeed?

Research your worth to your employer

Before requesting a raise, research your company. Assess your worth to your company. Look at the profits you made or even the losses you might have incurred. Look at your department and calculate your present productivity against that of a predecessor, if possible. For example, if you work in customer service, have you been able to increase customer satisfaction?

138

Compare your worth with your competition

Research online what is your market value or what you would be worth to the competition. If you're not earning what you would in comparable companies or organizations, this will give you an advantage in negotiating a raise.

Arrange a meeting with your boss

Schedule a date and time to discuss your raise with your boss. Don't say you're going to request a raise; rather, say that you have something important to talk about and you'd like to set up a meeting to discuss it.

Before going into the meeting, write down the concrete reasons you deserve a raise and rehearse them to ensure a confident and convincing delivery. During the meeting, first state the facts you have researched before requesting a raise.

If your boss takes calls during the meeting or acts as though you need to rush through, ask to reschedule to a time when you can have their uninterrupted attention.

Don't beg, make demands, or threaten to quit

Don't beg your boss for a raise or threaten to quit. These may backfire because your boss may begin to have negative feelings against you.

State what you want

Specify a particular amount you would like to receive. Be reasonable but not conservative. Then raise it by at least fifty percent so you have some room to negotiate.

Negotiate your raise

If your boss consents to a raise but offers a smaller amount than what you requested, counteroffer with an amount higher than in the middle. Continue to negotiate until both you and your boss agree upon a suitable amount.

What if your boss says no?

Your boss may simply reject your request for a raise. One response is to complain about all the problems the company or organization is having and how it's not possible to squeeze out another dime because of it.

Or, you understand the problems at the company, but you have personal financial responsibilities too. Say it's not fair to penalize you for the company's problems, that you give the company your best effort, and expect to be fairly compensated.

Your boss may use the company's policies to bar you from getting a raise. Work with your boss to find ways around the policy or consider the reasons why you should be an exception to the rule.

Don't accept a symbolic raise

In lieu of a pay raise, your boss may offer a small token raise or perks such as the use of the company car or a corner office with windows. Don't accept it. This will start a pattern where you are willing to accept anything instead of the larger raise you want. Rather, tell your boss that it is insufficient and reiterate the amount you are looking for.

Take a promotion

One of the best ways to get a raise is to get a promotion. You can do this in three different ways.

First, you can move up in the organization to the next level. Secondly, you can take on more responsibility. You may need to eliminate lower function work to do this. And third, you can create a new job for yourself with a new title.

If you think your best bet is the third option, write out a job description before you go into the meeting. Detail what is lacking and provide a plan for solving the problem. Include things such as what your job would entail, time frames for accomplishing assignments, costs, and what you estimate the profits would be. Talk with your boss about supporting you, and then go up the chain of command to have your plan approved.

Do not take a promotion without a title or a raise

If your boss offers a promotion without a new title or a raise, turn it down immediately. Because you'll probably be expected to take on further responsibilities in addition to the work you're already doing. And this is not acceptable.

Tell your boss that a promotion is really not a promotion without a raise. If you're offered a new position, make sure it's with responsibilities that you accept and with a raise that is appropriate to the new title.

Points to remember when asking for a raise:

- Choose the right time for your request

- Ask after a big win

- Don't give an ultimatum

- Avoid giving too much personal information

Assertive questioning to get information

When attempting to get information out of your customers, friends, or family, the question's length and the format determine its assertiveness quotient.

Longer questions asked with intent or context can make the prospects feel pressured to respond a certain way. Getting right to the point, on the other hand, sounds more assertive.

Tips for asking assertive questions

Leave yourself out of it

Remove pronouns, including "me" and "I" around things you want. The assertive person asks for what they want and waits for the answer.

Don't indicate your dislike of prospective answers

Accept their answer and ask if there's anything you can collectively accomplish.

Choose your verb carefully

Telling your prospect, "I'd really like to meet your boss" is not a question and is aggressive. If you want to meet their manager, say "I'd love the chance to explain the benefits of our product to your boss. Would it be possible for us to meet?"

It's always best to stick to single-sentence questions and skip the upfront explanation.

Homework for you

1. What stops you from asking others what you want?

2. Do you really feel you deserve a pay raise? Then, why haven't you asked for it yet?

3. Are you asking your customers the right questions, and in the right way?

Chapter Summary

- Overthinking about what others will think prevents us from asking them for what we want.

- Before requesting others to change their behavior, establish empathy and respect for them. State your positive feelings followed by the problem and in the end, the goal or the request for the new behavior.

- When asking your boss for a pay raise or a promotion, first research and note down the facts that make you eligible for it. Schedule a direct meeting with your boss and state those facts before requesting a raise. Never beg for a raise or threaten to quit. State what you want clearly.

- Never ask lengthy questions from your prospects or questions that pressure them to answer in a certain way. Ask what you want and wait for the answer. Never give upfront explanations.

In the next chapter you will learn:

- How to exercise assertiveness in daily life

- How to be assertive at work

- How to practice assertiveness with family and in relationships

- How to stand up and speak for yourself

CHAPTER NINE

Assertiveness Everyday

Assertiveness in daily life

Everyone wants to be more confident, but not everyone knows how to be assertive. If you learn to be assertive, you can express yourself easily and have a better chance of getting what you want.

Here are seven simple ways to become more assertive:

1. Understand that assertiveness is a skill

2. Be respectful of those with whom you communicate. Pay attention to your body language as well as the words you say, and make sure they are congruent.

3. Understand and accept the differences between your point of view and the others' points of view.

4. Speak in a way that doesn't accuse or make the other person feel guilty. Be simple, direct, and concise, and state what you know to be true for you.

5. Use "I statements" to be assertive without coming across hostile.

6. Stay calm when expressing yourself.

7. Set boundaries for yourself that help you decide what you will and will not allow.

When faced with a demand, consider the following:

Everyone, including you, has the right not to accept the demand. You have the right to say "no" without justifying yourself.

When rejecting a demand, explain that it is the demand that is being rejected and not the person.

After rejecting the demand, stick to that decision. If you crumble under pressure, others will learn that you can be swayed. However, you have the right to change your mind if circumstances change.

When receiving criticism:

- Take time to decide if it's genuine or is there some other reason for it.

- Acknowledge any truthful elements of criticism, even if they are hard to accept.

- Don't respond by lashing back with counter-criticism.

- Avoid criticizing others. Instead, give constructive, albeit negative, feedback to change their behavior.

- When giving feedback, focus on the problem or situation rather than the person.

Complimenting is a positive way of giving support, showing approval, and increasing the other person's self-confidence. However, some people find the giving and receiving of compliments difficult or embarrassing.

When you are complimented, thank the person giving the compliment, and accept it, whether or not you actually agree with it. When giving a compliment, ensure it is genuine.

Assertiveness at work

To exercise assertiveness at work, follow these steps:

Recognize your value. Nurture a realistic and respectful perspective on your value as a person.

Know your rights at the workplace. The notices, employee policy manual, your job description, etc.

Know your boundaries to avoid stress and frustration.

Prepare and practice

Practice being assertive with your close relationships. Imagine what it might be like to communicate something difficult to your co-worker or your boss. Ask yourself:

What is my goal, what and how would I like to say it?

Act it out in your mind, playing out both the ideal scenario and the scenario that scares you the most. If you don't, when the moment comes, your nerves might get you tongue-tied and it can feel easier to give up.

Avoid using words like "hmm," "uh," "you know..." "well...," etc., that can make your speech sound unsophisticated, hesitant, or indecisive.

Control the volume of your voice.

Avoid degrading language

Now, let's apply these steps to a few situations in the workplace.

Situation #1: Getting the team behind your plan

Your team is in charge of launching a new advertising campaign, and you have a killer idea. You call a meeting to discuss how to get started and are excited to propose your idea.

δ **Passive Approach:** You wait for your boss to make the first suggestion. Then, you passively nod your head to all his suggestions rather than putting up your idea or even suggesting ways to improve upon his strategy.

● **Aggressive Approach:** You immediately pitch your "perfect" idea to all your teammates, and without taking a breath, start assigning tasks. If anyone suggests an alternative, you outwardly reject it.

● **Assertive Approach:** You present your idea and welcome suggestions from all the team members. As you listen to the various suggestions, you acknowledge their strong points and also assume a role in solving potential challenges.

With an assertive approach, you state your case in a way that acknowledges others' perspectives and backs up your ideas with factual reasoning, rather than emotions. You successfully contribute value to the conversation, but not at the cost of degrading other team members.

148

Situation #2: You've asked for a raise, but your boss isn't making any moves

After asking for a raise during a meeting with your boss, she says that you'll have to wait for another six months as the company is just not able to give raises right now. She assures that you'll be considered for a salary bump when the time is right.

δ **Passive Approach:** You swallow your disappointment and agree with your boss in the office. But later, when you go home, you complain about it for hours because you feel it's completely unjust.

δ **Aggressive Approach:** You inform your boss that you'll begin to look for opportunities at other companies where someone will treat you like you deserve to be treated.

δ **Assertive Approach:** You respect yourself and your need to be compensated fairly, and also understand your boss' reasoning. So you ask for more information on the company's future and define concrete goals and targets that you can review when you revisit your salary request again in the future.

Assertiveness in family and relationships

Establishing assertive communication with your family is far easier. It gives you the following benefits:

- Better emotional and mental health

- Improves your social and personal skills

- Better understanding and control over your emotions

- Improves your self-esteem and decision-making skills

- Leads to self-respect and earned respect from others

Here are some ways to foster assertive communication with your family:

Avoid comparisons

Parents should dissuade from comparing their children with others. For example, "John, you didn't complete your homework. You should be more like Harry, who completes all his homework before going to the playground."

Comparison generates insecurity and feelings of inferiority, resentment, and unhealthy competitiveness.

Be empathetic

Assertive communication starts with respect towards others. When all the family members understand how they all think and feel, it'll be easier to engage in a healthy dialogue.

Ask for an opinion

Let your children participate and have a voice in making decisions that affect them and the family. This boosts their self-confidence and they feel their opinions matter.

Express yourself

For children to express their feelings and thoughts to you, you must follow suit. Tell them about your day, your concerns, and your interests. Similarly, listen attentively when children have something to share with you. Give them advice, if required, rather than judging and scolding them. Never punish them for telling you the truth.

Stand up and speak up!

Every day you make dozens of little choices. Sometimes, it's easy to assert your ideas, while at other times, it seems better to go with the flow to avoid potential conflict.

However, if you let people walk all over you; it can increase your feelings of stress and anxiety, and eventually lessen your feelings of self-worth.

Learning to speak up for yourself will help you take charge of your life, believe in your power, and embolden you to reach for your dreams.

So use these ten simple, yet powerful, steps to stand up for yourself in any situation.

Practice being transparent and authentic

It takes practice, but if you learn to express yourself openly and honestly, you'll get into the habit of making yourself heard by others.

Take small but powerful steps

Start by taking small steps to stand up for yourself. Even learning to walk with confidence – head held high and shoulders back – will help you feel and appear more confident. Channel this confidence in day-to-day interactions. Did someone push you out of the line at the Metro? Politely ask them to move back.

When someone attacks, wait them out

You'll sometimes come across people who will try to walk all over you. Stay calm but assertive if someone tries to bully you. Don't cater to them, but also don't react with aggression.

Figure out what bothers you

It requires a ton of courage to face something or someone that's bothering you. But, if you face it, it empowers you to make it better and diminishes its control over you. People can't read your mind; you have to vocalize your concerns.

Clarify before attacking

It's tempting to take a self-righteous stand, especially when the other person seems to be entirely in the wrong. But, resist your urge to react with emotion. Instead, take a breath and calmly explain your perspective to them. Avoid combative tones or accusatory words.

Practice, practice, and practice

Once you start getting the hang of it, practice assertiveness in situations where you need to stand up for yourself.

Be deliberate in voicing your concerns

Stand up for your time. Push back when appropriate or respectfully disengage with people or situations that submerge your schedule.

Remember, no one can invalidate your feelings, thoughts, and opinions. Learning to stand up for yourself won't happen overnight. It takes time to get comfortable with assertiveness. While you are in the learning stage, imagine that you are an actor learning to play a new role. Imagine that you are the most assertive person you know. So how will you handle yourself in a difficult situation?

So what about you?

1. Do you understand "assertiveness" now?

2. Do you feel confident in saying no? In expressing yourself? In asking for what you want?

3. Are you better equipped to stand up and speak for yourself now?

Chapter Summary

- Assertiveness is a skill that can be practiced and learned.

- Be respectful of those with whom you communicate. Understand and accept the differences between your and other's points of view. Stay calm when expressing yourself. Use "I statements" to be assertive without being hostile.

- Set boundaries for yourself.

- Recognize your value, know your rights at the workplace, speak in a clear, direct language, and avoid degrading words to sound assertive.

- Express yourself, ask for other's opinions, and be empathetic to exercise assertiveness in family and relationships.

- Take small but powerful steps to stand up and speak for yourself.

FINAL WORDS

Success at work and in relationships depends on your communication. Your style of communication should be such that it allows you to express, ask, and receive what you want in life.

There are three styles of communication – passive, aggressive, and assertive. But, it's only the assertive style that empowers you to be a winner in life. Passive communication makes you weak, submissive, and allows others to take advantage of yours. An aggressive style, on the other hand, makes you come across as domineering, haughty, and indifferent to others' feelings, thoughts, and opinions.

Assertiveness is the only way of communication that keeps your interests and those of others in perfect balance. You neither consider your own thoughts and feelings to be superior to others nor give in to other's perspective and demands unnecessarily. Both hold equal value for you.

By using an assertive style of communication in your day-to-day life, you improve your self-esteem, feel more confident, make better decisions, feel respectful about yourself, and gain others' respect, too. You can establish healthy and long-lasting relationships at work and with friends and family.

However, our own fears and assumptions pose a hindrance to learn and practice the skill of assertive communication. We believe that assertiveness will land us in conflict with our loved ones, colleagues, and peers, and we'll lose their love and appreciation. But the opposite is actually true. You'll gain more respect from others when you respect yourself and stand up for yourself, your rights, thoughts, feelings, and opinions.

Be curious to learn new things and be open to new experiences in life. Take care of how you present yourself to others. How you talk, your tone, clothes, and even your body language. Your body language speaks volumes about your self-confidence. It's an important aspect of assertive communication to be aware of.

Learning the skill of assertive communication starts with building a positive self-image. Have a rational and positive perspective of your abilities, skills, and strengths. This makes you feel empowered; the power to set meaningful goals in life and lay out the path to achieving them. You are unique and so is your contribution to this world. No one else can contribute the way you can. But, to realize this power of yours, you need to think positively about yourself.

By learning the assertive style of communication, you'll create in yourself the following qualities:

- Expressing your needs and ideas clearly, directly, and without guilt
- Standing up for your own rights and those of others
- Conveying your feelings to others with confidence
- Self-reliance and independence

- Persistence in complex situations

- Great analytical skills

- Positive attitude at all times

- Taking pride in your accomplishments

- Having the courage to dream and develop the skills needed to turn them into reality

To practice the assertive style of communication, you must know what you want, ask for it, and finally, get it. It's as simple as that.

Assertive communication involves three components:

1. Saying "no" at the right time and in the right way. It's a part of setting healthy boundaries for yourself and lets others know what you'll accept and what you won't; be it their behavior or their demands. Setting boundaries is crucial for you to conserve your emotional energy, give yourself a space to grow, improve your self-esteem and relationships, and avoid letting others manipulate you; in business, work, or personal relationships. You not only set yours but also honor others' limits if they've set them.

2. Clearly and confidently expressing how you feel about yourself and others' behavior towards you. You take complete responsibility for your feelings without blaming or accusing the other person. You make direct eye contact and use "I

statements" in a quiet voice and firm tone to deliver your message to others.

3. Asking others for what you want without losing your dignity and being empathetic and respectful towards others' needs, feelings, and opinions.

And the best part?

Assertive communication can be used in everyday life; at work, with family, and in your relationships. If you wish to succeed in life, create healthy relationships, or gain more respect from others, learn how to be assertive. This is one skill that can transform you into a winner.

I have outlined the exact steps you need to take to learn the skill of assertive communication, and how to apply it to your life. So, practice these steps and design the life you want.

RESOURCES

Assertiveness | Psychology Today. (n.d.). Retrieved November 20, 2019, from https://www.psychologytoday.com/us/basics/assertiveness

Thackray, V. (2016, November 11). 7 revealing facts about the psychology of assertiveness - PostiveChangeGuru.com. Retrieved November 20, 2019, from https://positivechangeguru.com/psychologists-assertive-you/

Choosing Your Communication Style | UMatter. (n.d.). Retrieved November 20, 2019, from https://umatter.princeton.edu/respect/tools/communication-styles

The 4-Types of Communication Styles. (n.d.). Retrieved November 20, 2019, from https://www.linkedin.com/pulse/20140626185020-15628411-the-4-types-of-communication-styles

Liyanage, S. (2015, July 21). Assertive Communication. Retrieved November 20, 2019, from https://www.slideshare.net/SamithaLiyanage1/assertive-communication-50744208

10 Benefits of Being More Assertive. (n.d.). Retrieved November 20, 2019, from http://www.magforliving.com/10-benefits-of-being-more-assertive/

9 Advantages of Assertiveness. (n.d.). Retrieved November 20, 2019, from https://threeinsights.net/book/9-advantages-of-assertiveness/

Kumar, D. (2014, July 18). The Importance of Being Assertive in the Workplace. Retrieved November 20, 2019, from https://www.careeraddict.com/the-importance-of-being-assertive-in-the-workplace

The Importance of Assertive Leadership. (n.d.). Retrieved November 20, 2019, from http://www.leadershipexpert.co.uk/importance-assertive-leadership.html

2011-2019, C. Skillsyouneed. C. (n.d.). Why People Are Not Assertive |

SkillsYouNeed. Retrieved November 20, 2019, from
https://www.skillsyouneed.com/ps/assertiveness2.html

Three Barriers that Would Stop You from Being Assertive. (2018, November 16).
Retrieved November 20, 2019, from http://compasscenterforleadership.com/three-barriers-that-would-stop-you-from-being-assertive/

Metaperceptions: How Do You See Yourself? (n.d.). Retrieved November 20, 2019,
from https://www.psychologytoday.com/us/articles/200505/metaperceptions-how-do-you-see-yourself

Chan, D. (2016, April 16). Learning to see things from another's perspective,
Opinion News & Top. Retrieved November 20, 2019, from
https://www.straitstimes.com/opinion/learning-to-see-things-from-anothers-perspective

How to Be Yourself and Cultivate a Positive Self-Image. (n.d.). Retrieved November
20, 2019, from https://www.developgoodhabits.com/positive-self-image/

Self-Image - how you see yourself positive or negative. (n.d.). Retrieved November
20, 2019, from http://destinysodyssey.com/personal-development/self-development-2/self-concepts-self-constructs/self-image/

2011-2019, C. Skillsyouneed. C. (n.d.-a). Personal Empowerment | SkillsYouNeed.
Retrieved November 20, 2019, from https://www.skillsyouneed.com/ps/personal-empowerment.html

Campbell, S. (2017, January 31). 8 Steps to Personal Empowerment. Retrieved
November 20, 2019, from https://www.entrepreneur.com/article/288340

What Is Personal Empowerment?: Taking Charge of Your Life and Career. (n.d.).
Retrieved November 20, 2019, from
https://www.mindtools.com/pages/article/personal-empowerment.htm

Assertiveness Training: Empowerment - Empowered Life Solutions. (n.d.).
Retrieved November 20, 2019, from http://empoweredlifesolutions.com/healthy-living/assertiveness-training-empowerment/

Marsden, L. (2014, May 13). 4 Tips to be Assertive and Empower Your Life - Laurie Marsden. Retrieved November 20, 2019, from https://lauriemarsden.com/4-tips-assertive-empower-life/

how to be a lion: 7 steps for asserting yourself positively. (n.d.). Retrieved November 20, 2019, from https://www.positivelypresent.com/2010/05/how-to-be-a-lion.html

Tartakovsky, M. M. S. (2018, July 8). Assertiveness: The Art of Respecting Your Needs While Also Respecting Others' Needs. Retrieved November 20, 2019, from https://psychcentral.com/blog/assertiveness-the-art-of-respecting-your-needs-while-also-respecting-others-needs/

https://www.pennstatehershey.org/documents/1803194/10660403/OAW+Assertiveness+Training+1.pdf/9f8788f4-219d-4fc1-a034-24551034d840

Kass, A. (n.d.). Three Keys to Assertive Behavior. Retrieved November 20, 2019, from https://www.gosmartlife.com/marriage-intelligence-blog/bid/148841/three-keys-to-assertive-behavior

Leinwand, L. (2016, November 10). Why Is Saying 'No' So Important? Retrieved November 20, 2019, from https://www.goodtherapy.org/blog/why-is-saying-no-so-important-1110165

Doherty, Y. (2014, November 7). 10 Reasons You Should Speak Up And Never Regret Saying How You Feel. Retrieved November 20, 2019, from https://www.elitedaily.com/life/culture/speak-dont-regret-saying-feel/823735

Ramey, S. (2016, September 22). Assertive Communication: Express What You Feel Without... Retrieved November 20, 2019, from https://exploringyourmind.com/assertive-communication-express-feel-without-guilt/

How to be less emotional reactive. (2019, October 2). Retrieved November 20, 2019, from https://cassdunn.com/how-to-be-assertive/

Louise, E. (2019, February 19). Here's How to Ask For Help Courageously and Assertively! [2 Step Process] | The Launchpad - The Coaching Tools Company Blog. Retrieved November 20, 2019, from https://www.thecoachingtoolscompany.com/how-to-be-more-assertive-ask-for-help/

Why Is It Hard to Say "No" and How Can You Get Better at It? (n.d.). Retrieved November 20, 2019, from https://www.psychologytoday.com/us/blog/the-couch/201601/why-is-it-hard-say-no-and-how-can-you-get-better-it

Be More Effective - 12 Reasons Why It's So Hard to Say, "No." (n.d.). Retrieved November 20, 2019, from https://www.bemoreeffective.com/blog/12-reasons-why-its-so-hard-to-say-no/

https://www.cci.health.wa.gov.au/~/media/CCI/Consumer%20Modules/Assert%20Yourself/Assert%20Yourself%20-%2006%20-%20How%20to%20Say%20No%20Assertively.pdf

Dondas, C. (2019, June 16). 7 Tips on How to Say NO in an Assertive Way ... Retrieved November 20, 2019, from https://lifestyle.allwomenstalk.com/tips-on-how-to-say-no-in-an-assertive-way/

Wilding, M. L. (2018, July 8). 3 Ways to Say No and Be More Assertive in Business. Retrieved November 20, 2019, from https://psychcentral.com/blog/3-ways-to-say-no-and-be-more-assertive-in-business/

Chesak, J. (2018, December 11). The No BS Guide to Protecting Your Emotional Space. Retrieved November 20, 2019, from https://www.healthline.com/health/mental-health/set-boundaries#how-to-define-your-boundaries

Lancer, D. L. (2019, May 11). 10 Reasons Why Boundaries Don't Work. Retrieved November 20, 2019, from https://www.whatiscodependency.com/setting-boundaries-limits-codependency/

Lancer, D. L. (2019b, September 9). The Power of Personal Boundaries. Retrieved November 20, 2019, from https://www.whatiscodependency.com/the-power-of-personal-boundaries/

mindbodygreen. (2019, September 4). 6 Steps To Setting Good Boundaries. Retrieved November 20, 2019, from https://www.mindbodygreen.com/0-13176/6-

steps-to-set-good-boundaries.html

5 Golden Keys to Assertiveness and Setting Boundaries | Hypnosis Downloads. (2019, August 1). Retrieved November 20, 2019, from https://www.hypnosisdownloads.com/blog/5-golden-keys-to-assertiveness-and-setting-boundaries

Grohol, J. Psy. D. M. (2018, October 8). 10 Reasons You Can't Say How You Feel. Retrieved November 20, 2019, from https://psychcentral.com/lib/10-reasons-you-cant-say-how-you-feel/

Bennett, T. (2018, March 13). Why Is It So Hard to Express My Emotions? - Thriveworks. Retrieved November 20, 2019, from https://thriveworks.com/blog/hard-express-emotions/

» Assertiveness. (n.d.). Retrieved November 20, 2019, from https://www.emotionalintelligenceatwork.com/resources/assertiveness/

admin. (2019, November 20). The difference between confidence and assertiveness. Retrieved November 20, 2019, from http://buildyp.blogspot.com/2012/05/difference-between-confidence-and.html?m=1

A Simple Way to Be More Assertive (Without Being Pushy). (2018, January 31). Retrieved November 20, 2019, from https://hbr.org/2017/08/a-simple-way-to-be-more-assertive-without-being-pushy

Sheffield, T. (2015, November 6). How To Ask For What You Want & Be More Assertive. Retrieved November 20, 2019, from https://www.bustle.com/articles/122147-how-to-ask-for-what-you-want-be-more-assertive

Assertive Requests: Be more persuasive and diplomatic. (n.d.). Retrieved November 20, 2019, from http://web.csulb.edu/%7Estevens/assert%20req.html

Foolproof Ways to Use Assertiveness to Request a Raise. (n.d.). Retrieved November 20, 2019, from https://www.selfgrowth.com/articles/foolproof-ways-to-use-assertiveness-to-request-a-raise

Hoffman, J. (n.d.). The Secret to Asking Sales Questions Assertively, Not Aggressively. Retrieved November 20, 2019, from https://blog.hubspot.com/sales/asking-sales-questions-assertively-not-aggressively

Daskal, L. (2018, June 20). 7 Powerful Habits That Make You More Assertive. Retrieved November 20, 2019, from https://www.inc.com/lolly-daskal/7-powerful-habits-that-make-you-more-assertive.html

2011-2019, C. Skillsyouneed. C. (n.d.-a). Assertiveness in Specific Situations | SkillsYouNeed. Retrieved November 20, 2019, from https://www.skillsyouneed.com/ps/assertiveness-demands-criticism-compliments.html

Sese, C. (2018, April 19). 6 Tips for Being More Assertive at Work. Retrieved November 20, 2019, from https://www.goodtherapy.org/blog/6-tips-for-being-more-assertive-at-work-0113155

How to Be Assertive and Get What You Want at Work. (2013, June 20). Retrieved November 20, 2019, from https://money.usnews.com/money/blogs/outside-voices-careers/2013/06/20/how-to-be-assertive-and-get-what-you-want-at-work

Wilding, M. (2019, June 5). How to Be More Assertive at Work (Without Being a Jerk). Retrieved November 20, 2019, from https://www.themuse.com/advice/how-to-be-more-assertive-at-work-without-being-a-jerk

Lica, A. (2019, August 18). Assertive Communication with Your... Retrieved November 20, 2019, from https://exploringyourmind.com/assertive-communication-with-your-family/

Becoming Assertive? 4 Reasons Your Family Won't Like It. (n.d.). Retrieved November 20, 2019, from https://www.arenewedlife.com/becoming-assertive-4-reasons-family-wont-like/

Are You Too Nice? 7 Ways to Gain Appreciation & Respect. (n.d.). Retrieved November 20, 2019, from https://www.psychologytoday.com/us/blog/communication-success/201309/are-you-too-nice-7-ways-gain-appreciation-respect

Hutchison, M. (2015, August 6). 6 Assertive Ways To Get The Respect You DESERVE. Retrieved November 20, 2019, from https://www.yourtango.com/experts/moira-hutchison/how-gain-respect-others

Patel, D. (2018, November 9). 10 Powerful Ways to Stand Up for Yourself in Any Situation. Retrieved November 20, 2019, from https://www.success.com/10-powerful-ways-to-stand-up-for-yourself-in-any-situation/

Steber, C. (2019, June 12). 11 Little Ways To Stand Up For Yourself Every Day, No Matter What. Retrieved November 20, 2019, from https://www.bustle.com/articles/169607-11-little-ways-to-stand-up-for-yourself-every-day-no-matter-what

How to Speak Up for Yourself with Wisdom and Courage. (n.d.). Retrieved November 20, 2019, from https://www.psychologytoday.com/us/blog/prescriptions-life/201809/how-speak-yourself-wisdom-and-courage

Galinsky, A. (2017, February 17). How to speak up for yourself. Retrieved November 20, 2019, from https://ideas.ted.com/how-to-speak-up-for-yourself/

YOUR FREE GIFT IS HERE!

Thank you for purchasing this book. As a token and supplement to your new learnings and personal development journey, you will receive this booklet as a gift, and it's completely free.

This includes - as already announced in this book - a valuable resource of simple approach and actionable ideas to mastermind your own routine towards a more calm and confident way to tackle your everyday.

This booklet will provide you a powerful insight on:

- How to formulate empowering habits that can change your life

- Masterminding your own Power of 3

- Just the 3 things you need to drastically change your life and how you feel about yourself

- How to boost your self-esteem and self-awareness

- Creating a positive feedback loop everyday

You can get the bonus booklet as follows:

To access the secret download page, open a browser window on your computer or smartphone and enter: bonus.gerardshaw.com

You will be automatically directed to the download page.

Please note that this bonus booklet may be available for download for a limited time only.

Made in the USA
Monee, IL
08 July 2021